Divine Insights from Human Life

Eva Peck

© 2013 by Eva Peck

All rights reserved
Except for any fair dealing permitted under the Copyright Act, no part of this book may be reproduced by any means without prior permission of the author and publisher.

Artwork and photography: Jindrich Degen
Graphic design: Eva Peck

Cover art: Jindrich Degen
Cover design: Eva Peck

Bible quotes and paraphrases taken from the HOLY BIBLE, NEW INTERNATIONAL VERSION. Copyright © 1973, 1978, 1984 by International Bible Society. Used by permission of Zondervan Publishing House. All rights reserved.

National Library of Australia Cataloguing-in-Publication entry

Author: Peck, Eva, author.

Title: Divine insights from human life / Eva Peck.

ISBN: 9780987500328 (paperback)

Subjects: Spiritual life.
           Christian life.

Dewey Number: 248.8

The book can be purchased online through:
www.heavens-reflections.org or www.pathway-publishing.org

Dedicated to
all who desire to make their world a better place
and to perceive the transcendent.

Other Books by the Same Author

Divine Reflections in Times and Seasons
Divine Reflections in Natural Phenomena
Divine Reflections in Living Things

Co-author of:
Pathway to Life – Through the Holy Scriptures
Journey to the Divine Within – Through Silence, Stillness and Simplicity

Acknowledgments

First, I would like to thank the Great God for enabling, inspiring and blessing this publication.

I must also thank my husband, Alex, for his encouragement and support. He is always ready to help with editing and to give helpful advice. Without his valuable input, this book would not have come out as it has.

In addition, I want to thank my father, Jindrich Degen, for allowing me to use three of his artistic creations and for his input on the graphics.

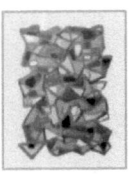

Contents

Preface 9

PART ONE: WISDOM FROM LIFE 13

The Phone Gift 15
    Instructions for Life 16
    Relating to God and Others 17

Lessons from the Stock Market 19
    Past Gives Clues to the Future 19
    Following Natural Instincts May Not Always Be the Best 20
    The Overall Trend Is Up 21
    Setbacks Can Have Unexpectedly Positive Outcomes 23
    Dark Times Don't Last Forever 24
    Need for Time and Patience 24
    Earthly and Heavenly Treasures 25

Reflections on a Computer Crash 28
    Real and Potential Losses 29
    Decisions and New Experiences 30
    Fear and Negative Anticipation 32
    Human and Divine Product Key 34

On Law and Order 37
    Purpose of Rules and Laws 38
    Post-Modern Thinking 40
    Biblical Law and its Implications 41
    Considering the Consequences 43
    What About Seemingly Nonsensical Laws? 44

How Not to Make Things Worse 46
    Thinking 47
    Communication 49
    Actions 51

Of Messy Houses and Loving Hearts 53
   Lessons Learnt – The Folly of Judging! 54

PART TWO: SPIRITUAL ANALOGIES FROM LIFE 57

Birth 59
   The Wonder of Life's Beginning 59
   Spiritual Parallels with Prenatal Development 60
   Special Births 65
   The Firstborn 67

Royal Wedding 69
   Wedding as a Biblical Metaphor 71
   The Marriage of Jesus Christ 72

Death of Two Young Men 75
   Death of Another Young Man 75
   Hope in the Face of Death 77

Freeing the Prisoners 79
   A Captive World 79
   About the Captor 81
   How the World Is Imprisoned 82
   Our Responsibility and Way Out 84
   Hope of Ultimate Liberation 85

Coming to Life on Facebook 87
   Spiritual Analogies 88
   The Wedding Banquet 90
   Those Not at the Banquet 92

About the Author 95

More About the Author's Other Books 96

Other Resources 98

About the Artist 100

About Pathway Publishing 101

Preface

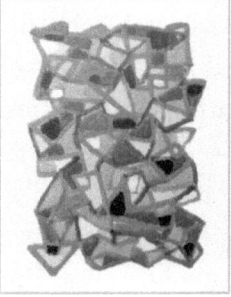

Recently, when I was going through my father's diverse collection of abstract paintings, one of them caught my attention as a fitting image of what this book is about. I chose it for the cover, as it inspired the following analogies and insights about life.

At birth, in some ways, each of us starts life like an artist standing before a blank canvas, sheet of paper, board, or another type of background material on which a piece of art can be created. For the duration of our earthly existence, we will be creating a picture of our life which will also leave an imprint on those around us. Initially, it will not be clear what the picture is going to be – the design and images will continue to emerge as time goes on.

Symbolically, the picture may be formed with paint, pastel or ink, among others, for a two-dimensional piece of art. Or, it may be composed of pieces of paper, wood, or other materials and objects to form a three-dimensional collage or mosaic. It may even become a beautifully decorated vase or bowl, or a statue made of marble, wood or metal. Indeed we are all artists, but instead of the canvas and paint or other materials, the media of life are our bodies, minds and spirits creating our experiences and fashioning our lives. Though we all have common human experiences, each of us is also unique. In addition, everyone has both special gifts and certain liabilities, as well as a different style. As a result, every person will create a reality unlike anyone who has ever lived or will live.

A hidden and mysterious dimension to the art piece of our life is that of the transcendent Divine. I believe that a guiding Hand works behind the scenes, though often not perceivable by us. While we have free will and choose our paths, which in turn lead to certain outcomes, there are times we are guided or led into situations that shape us and change the course of our lives in ways that we would have never expected or selected.

Some compare life to a divinely woven tapestry, that from below (our human perspective) looks like a tangled mess, but from the top (divine perspective) is a stunning design of awesome beauty – which while in our physical existence we can't perceive because of our limited senses. Ultimately, in God's perfect plan, whatever happens in this life will be for the good of ourselves and all others, even though it may not appear so at the time.[1]

The cover painting also conveys to me the idea of life as a series of experiences, coming in various shapes and colours, that make us what we are – and we will be changing and growing till the last "brushstroke" is placed or the last breath exhaled. The various shapes could represent different types of experiences, and the colours within them could picture the nature of these experiences. For example, the browns and blacks might be difficult or even traumatic experiences; the bright colours positive or edifying experiences; and the whites and yellows highs and special insights. Some of life's events may be both challenging and enlightening, as seen by the light and dark colours side by side. The yellow background could portray "blank spaces" yet to be filled before our life ends.

My father's painting, then, symbolically portrays what this book is about – it consists of several patches from the mosaic of

---

[1] See Romans 8:28

my life with reflections on the wisdom and/or spiritual insights that have been gleaned from the various incidents. The book has two parts – *Wisdom from Life* and *Spiritual Analogies from Life*.

The experiences in the first part of the book, *Wisdom from Life*, each include a challenge or a question, and then suggest scriptural principles for how to effectively deal with such a situation. No "best way" or "the way" is given as each person and their circumstances are different. However, the wisdom may be helpful when one is faced with similar dilemmas of life.

The second part, *Spiritual Analogies from Life,* consists of stories, followed by biblical analogies and metaphors with the intent of providing glimpses into spiritual realities. All names have been changed to protect the privacy of those involved.

For those who desire to learn more about the biblical teachings behind the conclusions, footnotes provide scriptural references.

I understand that the Divine is neither male nor female. However, to use the pronoun "it" seems inappropriate, therefore I am opting for the grammatical gender "he".

May the insights shared enrich you and help add bright colours to the mosaic of your life.

Eva Peck

PART ONE: WISDOM FROM LIFE

The Phone Gift

 The gift couldn't have been more timely and appropriate. After the last class before winter break, Ahmad, one of my husband's college students in Riyadh, Saudi Arabia, gave him a mobile phone which he no longer used, with enough money on it to last at least a month or two. It felt like God was providing for our needs in a country where public phones were all but nonexistent. With his new teaching responsibilities, Alex had not had time to call and arrange with Telecom for a landline connection at home. Coming to the office every day, he was managing without a phone and Internet at home. During the break, however, it would have been difficult.

Being new in the country, having to wait for his residency card (needed to get the phone connection at home), and not even knowing exactly what to do to get the phone connected – it was not unusual to be given three or more different answers to any "how to" question – all these factors made that little mobile precious.

The totally unexpected gift indeed helped in numerous ways. Getting the landline and Internet connected, calling the maintenance department to solve a hot water problem, and being able to be contacted are just a few examples. However, not having received an instruction manual with the phone and lacking experience with mobiles caused us some, thankfully not too serious, problems.

A few weeks after being given the mobile, we visited a phone shop and asked some questions about our particular model. The attendant kindly gave us an instruction manual for a similar model, which would have enabled us to figure out most of the functions on our phone. But being busy with work, we didn't read the instructions till about four months later after struggling with writing text messages, getting tangled up in the various options, and experiencing more than one frustration. This brought to mind the following analogy.

Instructions for Life

God has given us the gift of life with amazing bodies, minds and abilities. We walk, run, see, hear, smell, feel, think, and perform countless other functions. At the subconscious level, our body organs perform thousands of tasks, far surpassing the abilities of the most sophisticated computers. There are built-in warning systems (pain), back-up systems (compensation by other organs), defence systems (immunity), repair systems (healing), information processing (nerve paths and energy flow between organs), input (receiving stimuli through the senses or intuitively), output (response to stimuli) – the list could go on and on. In addition to this, we also operate in networks – family, friends, and other people in the society around us. Like a sophisticated computer that can work individually as well as in a network, do we also come with instructions?

I believe that, yes, the Creator God has given us, by revelation, instructions on how to use and maintain this precious gift of life in good working order, and how to interact with others without undue difficulties and a minimum of frustration. Unfortunately, however, just like my husband and I left our phone instruction manual on the shelf for months before reading it and finding more specifically how the mobile worked, many people have also not read and applied the divine instructions in a way that would have saved them needless suffering.

The instructions that the one God has provided are various inspired writings, which provide guidelines on how to successfully live. They include the Holy Scriptures (Old and New Testaments of the Bible), the Koran, the Four Noble Truths, the Eightfold Path, the Tao Te Ching, the Vedas, the Upanishads, and other sacred literature. Although written specifically for people in different times and places, these writings overlap on many points and contain much that is universally applicable to all humans, no matter when and where they live. Principles and guidelines are given on how to relate to the Creator or Source of our being, how to get on with fellow humans, how to think correctly, how to discern between beneficial and harmful emotions and actions, how to deal with life's conflicts and challenges, as well as how to ultimately receive eternal life. Some specific examples from the Bible follow.

Relating to God and Others

As far as relating to the Divine, the Source of all that exists, the Sacred Scriptures exhort to love God with all our mind, heart and soul. This sums up the first four of the Ten Commandments – letting God be uppermost in life, avoiding idol worship, using the divine name reverently, and setting aside time for worship. Other passages encourage heartfelt obedience and willing service to the Divine, thereby not grieving the Holy Spirit.[2]

Concerning relationships with others, the Bible (and other inspired writings) counsels to love our neighbour as ourselves and to apply the "Golden Rule" of treating others as we would like to be treated. Specifically, this includes truthfulness, forgiveness, reconciliation, honest work, edifying communication, service, as well as kindness and compassion. We are also taught that it is more blessed to give than to receive.[3]

---

[2] Matthew 22:37; Exodus 20:1-11; Deuteronomy 6:5; Ephesians 4:30.
[3] Matthew 7:12; James 2:8; Acts 20:35; Romans 13:8; Ephesians 4:25-32

Traditionally, marriage and family have been regarded as the building blocks of a society. For these to work as harmoniously as possible, the Scriptures give the following words of wisdom: for husbands and wives to love, respect and submit to one another; for parents to not exasperate and frustrate their children; and for children to obey and honour their parents.[4]

In addition, the Holy Scriptures counsel to think on what is good and uplifting, to maintain faith and hope, to avoid prolonged anger and bitterness, and to forgive rather than bear grudges.[5] The importance of right thinking and the connection between negative emotions and physical illnesses have been recognized by Western science only relatively recently, though in the East, this has been understood for centuries, if not millennia.

Like my husband and I with our mobile phone, without specific know-how and understanding, humans manage to function and survive, albeit with many frustrations and struggles. However, if we read, ponder and apply the divine instructions inspired by our Maker that have been preserved for us over millennia, we will discover a fuller, more enlightened life on the earth, and in the future a life without end.[6]

---

[4] Ephesians 5:21-28, 6:1-4
[5] Philippians 4:7-8; Ephesians 4:29-32, 5:4
[6] John 10:10; Romans 2:7-8; Galatians 6:8; 1 John 5:20

Lessons from the Stock Market

The global stock market dropped drastically on this particular day in 2008 and in the next few days and weeks continued in a steep decline. In its sensationalism, seemingly delighting in the bad news, the media got us off balance. There had been talk of a worldwide recession and our own investment had decreased significantly in only a few months. Not fully understanding the longer-term dynamics of the stock market but depending on the investment for our living costs, we became very nervous and troubled – almost to the point of panic. An informative and reassuring talk with our financial advisor put our minds at ease. From it also came the following insights for life in general and the Christian life in particular. I believe they can provide hope when we encounter difficult times – both financially and in other ways.

Past Gives Clues to the Future

The stock market responds to multiple and complex factors both nationally and globally, including the mood created by the ubiquitous media. No one can therefore predict the exact movement in the market and short-term predictions often turn out incorrect. However, longer-term past trends do indicate future trends.

Similarly, specifics in our own life cannot be predicted, but experiences of and lessons learned by our predecessors give us clues to our future. Since we all share in a common humanness, this applies particularly to our physical, psychological and spiritual development and what accompanies each stage. For example, we can see those who are our seniors aging and know through their experiences what challenges we may have to face down the line. On both collective and individual levels, it holds true that history tends to repeat itself and those who don't learn from the mistakes of others (or one's own) are destined to repeat them.[7]

Many who have reached out to a Higher Power in their time of need have found from their experience of help, providence and deliverance from trouble that it gives them hope for the same happening in future difficult situations. Also, God's written Word contains reassuring accounts of people who have been helped in times of crisis, as well as promises of divine provision and deliverance. Some were miraculously saved in the midst of fatal situations.[8] Others have recognized God as the Source of their comfort and hope – even if they were ultimately not miraculously delivered.[9]

Following Natural Instincts May Not Always Be the Best

When the stock market is down, the natural inclination is to get out of it by selling. This is, however, not always the best response, for one will invariably suffer loss. Rather, financial advisors counsel to do the opposite – invest more at such times, because when the shares are down, they will, based on past trends, again rise and when that happens, the investment will turn out profitable. (Of course, if a particular company we have invested in is facing serious and irreversible problems and likely

---

[7] Ecclesiastes 1:4-9; 9:1-3; 1 Corinthians 10:11-13
[8] For example, Daniel 3:1-30; 6:3-24
[9] Genesis 49:25; Psalms 10:14; 27:1-3; 54:4; 70:5; 118:5-14; Philippians 4:19; Ephesians 3:20; Hebrews 11

bankruptcy, it would be wise to sell that stock while there is still some value in it.)

Humanly speaking, to those who have not experienced it, the Christian way of life may on the surface seem like a poor investment. One may need to give up certain things held dear, endure ridicule, and even suffer persecution. At times, the challenges may feel overwhelming even for believers. One can get very angry with God for their predicament, and even be tempted to give up on God and quit. Yet, it is through perseverance that success will be reached.[10] In the overall scheme of the divine plan, the spiritual benefits now and especially those promised in the future will far exceed any hardships suffered.[11]

The Overall Trend Is Up

It is normal for the stock market to fluctuate over the short term with smaller or larger ups and downs, but over the long term, its trend is overall upward. In the history of the stock market, good years with positive returns have outnumbered bad years, although the timing of good or bad years is often hard to predict.

Also, two variables interact in stock market trends. Growth in the value of shares reflects investor confidence which is influenced by events and news reporting of the time. Dividends reflect the profits of individual companies and are subject to less fluctuation as business continues in spite of a disaster or civil war on the opposite side of the globe. So even when the value of shares is down, dividends usually continue.

Likewise, human life is a series of peaks and valleys, successes and failures, gains and losses, joys and sorrows. However, in the long run, especially for those whose lives are aligned with the

---

[10] Luke 8:15; Hebrews 10:36; James 1:12; 5:11
[11] 2 Timothy 3:12; Mark 10:23-30; 2 Corinthians 4:17-18; Romans 8:18

positive laws of the universe – such as love, kindness, generosity, gratitude, and looking to God – life is overall good. Interestingly, even those whose lives may appear hard and miserable from a Western perspective are often happy and content. (There are, of course, also many in various parts of the world who live in grinding poverty, oppression, hunger and sickness for whom the present life is not good.)

Generally speaking, for most people, as time goes on, grief from losses diminishes and hardships are seen as learning and growth opportunities. Christians trust the scriptural promises that God will never leave nor forsake them and that in the long run, all things will work together for good.[12]

While human life is unpredictable and to a large extent uncontrollable, it is in the hands of a benevolent Creator God – or as some prefer to say, we live in a friendly universe. Even though we don't understand why many things happen and why even good people suffer unjustly, we can trust that God's overall intent is not to hurt or destroy humans, but rather to give them life for eternity – far better than they had imagined or at the best of times experienced.[13]

The overall trends of the stock market are the same worldwide – short-term ups and downs and a long-term upward trend. They may differ in the timing of the downward trends and what sparked them off, as well as in the timing of the recoveries.

In a similar way, all people overall experience common problems and ups and downs. The difficulties may vary in their causes and specific details, but with God in all things – even if unseen and unrecognized – the downward trend is moderated

---

[12] Romans 8:28; Hebrews 13:5-6
[13] 2 Thessalonians 3:3; Romans 2:6-7

and overall, human potential, with the hope of liberation, salvation and eternal life, is upward.[14]

Setbacks Can Have Unexpectedly Positive Outcomes

A serious downturn with net losses in the stock market is often followed by a sharp upturn with above-average gains. This of course takes several years and it is hard to predict how many. Based on past records, these transition years are characterized by considerable volatility, but once there is a turning point in the downward trend, there is usually a period of good positive growth.

In life, this can also be the case. A crippling accident, stroke, or another serious setback or tragedy can ultimately result in personal growth and life's achievement that would have otherwise not occurred. What initially brought deep despair may be retrospectively viewed as a blessing and a stepping stone to great service. Consider the lives and accomplishments of people like Joni Eareckson Tada or Nick Vujicic,[15] both with severe disabilities. Hardships teach us lessons and help us develop character, gain wisdom, and feel compassion. In a way analogous to parents disciplining their growing children out of concern for their present and future wellbeing, God too uses trials to help us learn what we otherwise wouldn't and to purge undesirable traits from our lives – all this motivated by divine love.[16]

---

[14] 1 Corinthians 10:13; 1:9; 1 Peter 5:8-10
[15] For inspiring biographical information on both individuals, you can check http://www.joniandfriends.org/jonis-corner/jonis-bio/ and http://www.christianpost.com/news/limbless-evangelist-nick-vujicic-honeymoons-with-new-wife-in-hawaii-69883/ among many other online references.
[16] Psalms 94:12-13; Hebrews 12:5-13; Revelation 3:19

Dark Times Don't Last Forever

Based on past trends, every market drop, including the disastrous 1929 crash, has been followed by a recovery – maybe not always quick, but eventually an upturn and subsequent growth have always come.

Similarly in life, one can be confident that a dark period will not last forever, even though when in the midst of it, there may seem no way out of a desperate situation. Hope and faith are important in any crisis – hope in deliverance or recovery from the seemingly hopeless situation, and faith that there is a loving God who has our welfare in mind and will step in when we recognize that there is nothing more we can do by ourselves. Those who lose hope may just give up on life, whereas people with hope and faith have survived incredible odds against them.[17]

Need for Time and Patience

Stock market investment cannot be correctly evaluated over a short-term period – one would arrive at either a too pessimistic or a too optimistic picture. It is the average over several years or even decades that represents an accurate view. It is important to invest with a longer-term view and investors then need to patiently wait for their profits.

In a parallel manner, circumstances in life, a person's contribution to society, or events in history are also hard to evaluate as they are happening. Only retrospectively can their impact be seen more objectively. Christians also need to be patient and

---

[17] Romans 12:12; 15:4, 13; 2 Corinthians 1:10; 1 Thessalonians 1:3; 1 Timothy 5:5; 6:17

persevere in serving and doing good before receiving their spiritual and eternal rewards.[18]

Earthly and Heavenly Treasures

In this essay so far, I have sketched out in broad brush strokes how the stock market works and then drew some principles for life in general. These include learning from the past, thinking longer-term, being patient, and looking at setbacks as springboard to greater future success. This last section puts finances in a broader context of life beyond this life.

While financial resources are necessary for living, believers are warned of the pitfalls in becoming overly attached to monetary treasures. This is because the love of money tends to lead to greed and misplaced priorities.[19] Also, wealth by itself does not satisfy in the long run – those who pursue it in the hope of making them happy find that riches cannot buy true love or happiness. In addition, possessions are fleeting, and undue attachment to them brings disappointment and even despair when losses occur.[20] If you doubt this, consider the following, among other similar situations.

In 1923, a group of seven American financial giants gathered at a prestigious hotel in Chicago. Their combined wealth totalled more than the worth of the United States Treasury. Twenty-five years later, a check was made into how their lives had gone. The findings were not good – and indeed surprising. Of the seven extremely rich men, two died in poverty, two ended up in prison, and three committed suicide. In more recent times, billionaire Howard Hughes spent his last years as a sick recluse, and J. Paul

---

[18] 2 Thessalonians 3:5; James 5:7-8
[19] 1 Timothy 6:6-10, 17-19; Matthew 6:24; 13:22
[20] Proverbs 23:5; Psalms 62:10

Getty was reported in the press to have made the statement, "I'd give all my wealth for just one happy marriage."

A Wall Street Journal article described money as "an article which may be used as a universal passport to everywhere except Heaven, and as a universal provider of everything except happiness." Nonetheless, many believe that more money will make them happy, that if they won the lottery, all their problems would disappear. At best, a large amount of money brings only temporary happiness.[21]

Rather than relying on physical riches, we as people of God are to place our faith and trust in our Creator who promises to provide for all our needs and even fulfil many wishes and desires.[22] We are to seek heavenly treasures which may not always be clearly visible in this life but when they manifest, they will last for ever.[23]

The Holy Spirit is metaphorically referred to as a treasure in jars of clay (human bodies). It is a down-payment of salvation and eternal life – compared to a pearl of great value.[24] God has already given his Son Jesus Christ to save the world from the penalty of human sins. He has raised Jesus from the dead and thus conquered death and opened the way to enable a resurrection of others.

One day, all suffering and death will be done away with.[25] When that time comes, those who have invested into God's kingdom on earth will reap dividends beyond their wildest dreams. The heavenly "stock market" will continue to rise exponentially and forever without any dips.

---

[21] Information adapted from
http://www.swiftcreekbaptistchurch.com/Sermons/James5_01-6.pdf
[22] Philippians 4:19; 2 Corinthians 9:18; Matthew 7:7-11; James 1:17; 1 John 3:22
[23] Matthew 6:19-34; 2 Corinthians 4:18
[24] 2 Corinthians 4:7; Romans 8:11; Matthew 13:45-46
[25] John 3:16; 1 Corinthians 15:45-54; Revelation 22:1-4

The gains from today's stocks and bonds may provide a measure of capital which is necessary for living and sharing the good news of the present and future kingdom of God. The ultimate investment, however, is in divine stocks with unlimited dividends.

Reflections on a Computer Crash

I switched on my computer as usual, ready to begin work. That morning however, instead of the usual friendly blue-green display and familiar jingle, the screen remained black with rather foreboding white writing in the lower third. The message informed me that Windows (the environment necessary for all other programs to operate) couldn't be opened because a certain file was corrupted or missing. That of course didn't start the day on the right foot. Luckily I had been creating back-up copies of my files and so lost no work.

In the days and weeks prior to the crash, the computer gave no warning of malfunctioning or winding down – though being almost five years old, it wasn't altogether unexpected. However, computer users are advised that a serious malfunction or crash is never out of the realm of possibility. They are urged to back up all their work by creating extra copies on portable devices, so that if a problem occurs, files can be accessed on another computer or copied onto a new one.

We all get used to our routines and when something unexpectedly goes wrong, feelings of disappointment, frustration, disorientation, even anger, set in. This is especially true if we are task-oriented and like to be in control of life, which is of course to a large degree impossible. Suddenly, we're unable to do what we wanted, our schedule is upset, and we feel greatly inconvenienced and even overwhelmed. We realize how dependent we have become on the particular item and how much we have taken for granted. Anxiety and fear may arise as a result of not knowing what to do and how it will all work out.

After recovering from the shock of a non-functioning computer, my husband and I started thinking about the best course of action. What would be the wisest – seek a repairman or buy a new computer? A few phone calls to computer specialists quickly convinced us that in today's world of planned obsolescence and fast-changing technology, the computer was not worth fixing. We were told that most computers last for about three years and I was lucky with mine working for almost five. So with that consensus, we decided to go to town and buy a new computer.

What can be learned from a sudden and unwelcome change of circumstances? This essay explores the issues of loss, sound decision making, anticipation, as well as some spiritual analogies.

Real and Potential Losses

Realizing how much we take for granted until we lose something, one lesson is to appreciate what we have and to make the most of it while it lasts. Once it goes – and in a world of impermanence, it is guaranteed to come to an end sooner or later – there is no way back. This applies especially to relationships. Like the suddenly crashed computer hard drive, a person's life may irreversibly change or end without forewarning. Therefore it's important to express love, care, kindness and appreciation to loved ones and friends while we can, so that if something unexpected happens, unnecessary regrets will not pile up on top of our natural grief and sorrow. Losing family members or friends as a result of an accident or sudden fatal illness brings to the fore the painful realization of how short and fragile life is.[26]

---

[26] Psalms 39:5; 144:4; Job 7:7; 1 Corinthians 7:29-31; James 4:13-14; 1 John 2:17

Change is inevitable, but there may be no warning before it occurs. We all know the value of doing everything we can ahead of time and being prepared as much as is possible for what is likely to happen – though sometimes prior preparation is simply not possible. Luckily, I heeded the warnings of computer experts and most of my items were backed up. However, I know of friends and acquaintances that have lost precious amounts of work, even whole books. When we suffer loss, we quickly learn from our short-sightedness or negligence and seek to avoid future problems. It is of course even wiser to learn from the unfortunate mistakes of others and to act ahead of time whenever possible to avoid needless difficulties.[27]

Decisions and New Experiences

The decision to look for a new computer was relatively easy based on the consensus of opinion among the experts. Many decisions in life are not that simple. At times when gathering information, we receive conflicting input and can temporarily end up more confused than enlightened. Nevertheless, we still need to gain a good understanding of the issue, consider all aspects, know the options, and make as informed decision as possible. The wisdom books of the Holy Scriptures encourage getting extensive input as there is safety in abundant counsel. After we have gathered information and know what is involved, we are also promised divine wisdom for the decision, if we ask for it.[28]

Once in the shop, the next decision was which particular computer to buy. A range of laptops in a variety of prices was on display. The helpful young shop assistant promoted a payment scheme that would enable us to have a new up-to-date computer

---

[27] 1 Corinthians 10:6-10
[28] Proverbs 11:14; 15:22; 24:6; 2:6; James 1:5-6

every year or two. We realized, however, that in the end we would pay twice as much as what the computer was worth. Having rejected that option, we still had to decide on the best model – one that would hopefully function satisfactorily for more than just a year or two. Looking at all the possibilities, considering quality versus cost, and sorting out between facts and sales pitch, we finally decided on a middle-of-the-price-range laptop and also purchased additional warranty.

We all feel comfortable with what we have been used to, prefer what is predictable and easy to use, and tend to resist change. New technology, especially for mature-age users, is challenging and involves a learning curve – sometimes quite a steep one. I unpacked the computer and started reading the instruction manual. An insert full of cautions and warnings made me feel concerned and a little overwhelmed. One warning was about the possibility of a low-heat injury upon prolonged use. And indeed, after a day or two of using the touch pad, my index finger developed a red area. I started having doubts that this lovely model, which was not cheap, was the right one for me after all.

In life, we may find ourselves in new circumstances, even of our own choosing, that at first don't feel right. We may even doubt an important decision we had made. In times of such uncertainty, if we believe we have done the best under the circumstances and even sought divine guidance, it can be helpful to review what had led to the decision and to think through what other options there were. Re-establishing that we had made the best possible decision will put our minds at ease. Also important to realize is that it always takes time and patience to get used to new situations, as well as to make the necessary adjustments in one's thinking, perspective and way of acting.

After following the step-by-step setup instructions in the manual, I plugged the computer into the power outlet and switched it on. I waited in anticipation as the new Windows program, a version which I was unfamiliar with, was configuring itself over perhaps 20 minutes or more. During this time I was asked to choose my icon, password, and a few other things. Finally, the system was up and running, but still a little overwhelming with its differences from the program I was used to.

Fear and Negative Anticipation

Some aspects of the new computer setup proved easier than expected. Connecting to the Internet was quite straightforward, although in calling our provider for instructions, we had to wait about 15 minutes for customer service. We needn't have worried about finding an old setup CD as it was no longer needed. An inbuilt modem on the computer also automatically took care of programming the computer that was needed in the past. Getting Skype working again, even with all the contact addresses and phone numbers intact, was likewise easy, and so was reconnecting the printer. Gone were the days when a CD was required to download drivers – upon connecting the printer by a USB port, the needed drivers were automatically and swiftly downloaded and the machine was ready to use.

Activation of the writing and editing programs of Microsoft Office proved more of a challenge. Our user agreement allowed for three computers to use the software we had and it had only been used on two – therefore available for the new laptop. However, neither of the two numbers on the label corresponded to the 25 digits of the required product key code to activate the inbuilt version on the new computer. Customer support informed us that our software version may be too old to validate – although no time limit was given on the package. The next day, through a roundabout Internet search, I discovered a phone number which gave some hope. While the problem had not been resolved, at least there was a human technician to talk to. Several days later, after emailing photos of the original software product and receipt, I had to call back. A long sequence of being passed from one operator to another followed. After about 25 minutes on the phone however, the last operator created the needed product key based on a number on the CD, and I was finally set to go.

In life we sometimes anticipate problems and difficulties and then find to our pleasant surprise that we had worried needlessly. The Scriptures encourage us not to fear or fret unnecessarily and remind us of the futility of worry.[29] Even if situations turn out harder than we had thought, worrying about them ahead of time does not help, but rather depletes our energy needed for making decisions followed by constructive action.

Sometimes, much patience and perseverance is needed before we receive what we are entitled to or surmount a challenging situation. The important thing is to not give up. Just when we are about to quit, the desired outcome may be right around the corner – within easy reach.

A "can-do" attitude is also vital. If we believe that there is every reason we can succeed and tirelessly work toward that end, the positive expectation by itself will go a long way to achieving our goal. By contrast, fear and negative expectations will hold us back. Whatever our expectations are regarding personal success or failure, they will usually turn out to be correct!

---

[29] Matthew 6:25-34; Philippians 4:6-7; 1 Peter 5:7

Human and Divine Product Key

With a new computer, the Microsoft company gives users a Windows program (for example, Windows Vista or Windows 7) which works in the background, and a writing/editing program, Microsoft Office, which after a maximum of 25 uses needs a product key to properly activate it so that it can continue working. If the product key is not entered, the program is said to start losing its capabilities till eventually it becomes disabled. (I didn't reach this point to find out if it is true.)

The way the programs in a new computer are set up may give a faint reflection or glimmer of how God has wired human beings – which of course is in this life unfathomable, but maybe a few glimpses can be gained from this analogy. Perhaps a preliminary, temporary "program of divine nature" is set up in the heart of each person, but it only works partially until it is divinely activated. The original program seems to work somewhat in childhood, before the ego is fully developed with its self-will, pretentiousness, grasping, and ambitious striving. Interestingly, Jesus gave a little child as an example of certain qualities of the converted state. As time goes on, adults lose that childlike wonder, trust and innocence.[30]

Only God can create the right "product key", mixed with grace and suitable circumstances, among no doubt other factors of which we are unaware. When the "activation" by grace occurs, our minds are opened and our hard hearts softened. Through this transformation, we become aware of our ego pulling us toward grasping, controlling, holding on, and pursuing deceitful desires. We realize that this is not where our identity lies.[31]

Through intuitive knowledge from beyond our rational mind, we also become aware of God's love extended to us and expe-

---

[30] Matthew 18:1-5; 19:13-14; Mark 10:15; Luke 9:48; 10:51
[31] Ephesians 4:22; Jeremiah 17:9; Luke 24:45; Acts 16:14; Ezekiel 11:19; 36:26

rience a longing for God with a desire to respond to that love. The activated divine nature within – the Holy Spirit – is now glimpsed as the new self or true Self, the ground and source of our being, a transcendent mystery which is incomprehensible and indescribable, yet beckoning us. With our cooperation, it will start transforming the human nature (false self or old self) into the image of Jesus Christ and produce the fruit of the Spirit in our lives – love, joy, peace and goodness. We will have experienced a new birth, become a new creation, and now walk in newness of life.[32]

Not wanting to just throw away the old laptop, which was still in good condition, I thought that if I could get it working, it might be a useful back-up system, or I could even use it outside. Internet research suggested that the encountered problem was common and that one of several solutions might work. We tried them all, but unfortunately without success. We even tried a rescue CD that my husband had for his old laptop. After an initial spark of hope, it didn't work either. Later we found out from a computer specialist that the hard drive had become faulty and needed replacing.

Scriptures and experience show that while people have a great potential for good, there is also a basic flaw in the human "hard drive" – the heart. Ultimately, a new heart is needed – one that is receptive to God's gentle nudging and able to follow divine will. And this is exactly what the Scriptures promise – a coming time when for humanity collectively, the heart of stone will be replaced with a heart of flesh. All things will be made new and brought into harmony and unity with their divine source. All pain and suffering will cease and be forgotten. A new heaven and

---

[32] Romans 6:4; 2 Corinthians 5:17; Colossians 3:10; Ephesians 4:23-24; Galatians 5:22-25; 1 John 3:9; 4:7

earth will be established where all will live in full knowledge of God and in the bliss of everlasting divine presence.[33]

---

[33] Ezekiel 11:19; 18:31; 36:26-31; 37:1-14; Isaiah 11:1-12; 65:17-25; Romans 8:18-23; 1 Corinthians 15:22-28; 2 Peter 3:13; Revelation 21:1-4

On Law and Order

"Leaving at 6:15," announced Omar, the driver of our Middle Eastern college shopping bus. With the Muslim evening prayer, *Maghrib*, between 6:05 and 6:35 pm that night, this meant about half an hour to do the week's shopping. If we didn't get through the cashier checkout line before the beginning of the prayer time, we couldn't do it till after the prayer and be late for the bus.

Racing from one isle to the next and grabbing only the necessities, about two-thirds of the staff met the deadline. The others, knowing the bus wouldn't leave without them, did their shopping without rushing, or perhaps mismanaged their time and missed checking out before the prayer period by a minute or two. The irony was that those who strove to comply with the rule were penalized by having a rushed, unsatisfactory shopping experience, and then having to wait outside or in the bus for the rest of the group.

Based on situations like this, where following a rule seems to actually bring a penalty, this essay explores questions such as: What is the purpose of rules and laws? Does it pay to be law-abiding? Or, since sometimes it doesn't seem to make much difference, should we do as we please? What if the rules don't make sense or go against our conscience? What if many in our group disregard the rule anyway? What is the responsibility of a Christian in this respect?

Purpose of Rules and Laws

Overall, the purpose of law is to protect people from harm and allow them to live in peace.[34] This is true of the basic moral and ethical laws common to all the main religions, as well as belonging to the civil law codes of nations and civilizations. The fundamental moral law includes prohibition against killing, stealing, lying, and inappropriate sexual conduct. It also promotes marital faithfulness and fulfilment of obligations to parents – respect at all times, obedience in childhood, assistance to aging parents in adulthood. The last two are still generally upheld in religions, but are weakening in secular societies, especially in the West.

Both civil and religious legal codes have had volumes written elaborating on the basic moral and ethical principles, as well as other rules and regulations. Companies have their own rules, schools have rules, and even families develop rules. From our earliest childhood, we are surrounded by do's and don'ts, mostly intended to shield us from harm and to guide us in a way that will help us in life as we grow up and become independent of our parents. Specifically, their purpose is to instil habits that will make us responsible citizens able to positively contribute to society. Of course, not all rules are perfect or necessary, and some have been created with the aim to control rather than to help the ruled.

We also live on a planet and in a universe governed by physical laws. Examples include gravity and the laws of electricity. As children, for our own safety, we are strictly forbidden to put metal objects into electrical sockets or touch the hot stove. We soon learn that breaking certain laws doesn't pay – it causes pain and suffering. Few will attempt to defy the law of gravity by,

---

[34] 1 Timothy 1:9-10; 2:1-2; Romans 13:3-4

for example, jumping down from the top of a ten-storey building. Breaking of physical laws, even in ignorance, such as not understanding the laws of electricity, will more than likely exact a penalty.

Besides physical laws and moral laws, there also exist more subtle spiritual laws under the overall umbrella of the two great commandments of love to God and love to neighbour (including oneself)[35]. These include, among many others, respect for others as opposed to selfish indulgence; gratitude and contentment in contrast to greed and covetousness; and generosity as opposed to hoarding and stinginess. The negative aspects of these alternatives also bring penalties, especially over a period of time. One reason is that such behaviour as disrespect and greed goes against the principle of love and disrupts the needed balance and harmony – starting with our own bodies, minds and spirits and then spreading outwards to other people.

For example, we are all finding out how decades of exploitation and abuse of our natural environment (disrespecting the laws of nature as well as naked greed on the part of some) have caused various imbalances around the globe which in turn have resulted in unfavourable climate changes and increase in violent and destructive weather.

Spiritual laws may not be included in civil law books – you will not get jailed for coveting or being miserly, for instance, unless of course such attitudes result in stealing or fraud. These laws, however, are included in the sacred writings of all the main religions.[36] And there are built-in penalties for breaking them. For example, if we are continually dissatisfied with what we have and always want more, we can never be happy. We enter a vicious circle of always chasing after possessions – a bigger house,

---

[35] Matthew 22:36-40; 1 Corinthians 13:1-8
[36] See for instance Exodus 20:17; Romans 7:7-8; 13:9

better car, motor boat, custom-designed furniture, more money, and on and on – the desires never end, while happiness and contentment keep alluding us. The Buddhists correctly teach that desires for and attachments to physical things are among the chief causes of suffering.

In a nutshell, various laws exist to protect us from harm and to maintain peace and harmony in our environment. Breaking laws generally has negative consequences for the person doing it and often for others as well. This may not be obvious straight away, but will manifest over time if law breaking becomes a habit. The law of sowing and reaping (*karma* as this important principle is referred to in Buddhism) is another spiritual law operating throughout the universe.

Post-Modern Thinking

Western society particularly has changed markedly in the post-World War II era as we have transitioned from the era of modernism to post-modernism, a time of fewer if any absolutes and an ever-accelerating rate of change. In the last few decades, scientists have discovered that below the surface, at the sub-atomic level, nothing is as certain and solid as we had thought – even physical laws. This fluidity and uncertainty have carried over into the area of morals and ethics in terms of everything being relative to something else – which, of course is true to some extent, but has perhaps been extrapolated too far.

Many believe that no absolutes exist and that no one has the right to tell another person what to do. Everyone tends to do what is right in their own eyes. Young people are growing up in a time and environment where there is little recognition of a higher law. As a result, they are not learning to respect parents, teachers, or other figures of authority. In addition, corruption sometimes exists even in the police force, law courts, and government offices. It is therefore easy for all of us to even subconsciously absorb the same attitude of nonconformity which can be a subtle, or not so subtle, form of lawlessness.

Unfortunately this spreading atmosphere of indifference to or even contempt for law, especially in the West, has had some undesirable consequences. These have included increase in violent crimes, often committed by the young; disregard for public and private property such as theft, breaking in and vandalism; disrespect to others, often intensified if the other person is of a different race or beliefs; and even disregard for the sanctity of life, such as in the form of abortion. A counter-reaction to the lawlessness has been radical law enforcement, such as the imposition of *sharia* law in some Muslim countries.

Biblical Law and its Implications

In the Holy Scriptures (both in the Old and New Testaments), people are exhorted to be subject to laws as well as authorities, whom God instituted, be it police, employers, or local government officials, among others. Rebellion against those in charge is generally not condoned.[37] A valid reason for disobedience is when human law clearly conflicts with divine law – then the latter takes precedence.[38]

In view of this and the changing times, what should a Christian do if rules don't seem to make sense or fail to lead to the intended outcome? What if one is actually penalized for obedience in a setting where many disregard the rules? Here are some principles to consider.

Firstly, what we do shouldn't violate the two great commandments of love to God and love to neighbour (including love to oneself without being selfish). This surpasses all other laws and

---

[37] 1 Samuel 15:23; Numbers 26:9-10; Romans 13:1-7; Titus 3:1; Ephesians 6:1-9
[38] Exodus 1:15-21; Daniel 3:14-30; Acts 4:19; 5:29

rules. Secondly, we shouldn't violate our conscience. And thirdly, if we feel we must disobey, we should consider the consequences, count the cost, and if necessary, be prepared to pay the penalty.[39]

In this regard, we can also study the life of Jesus Christ, who never sinned and set us an example.[40] The gospels show that interestingly, even he had not always submitted to human rules and established customs, and unsurprisingly was criticised for it. For example, in a male-dominated culture, he wasn't afraid to break cultural taboos and freely conversed with women. He also accepted invitations from those whom others regarded as sinful, touched untouchable lepers, and even refused to keep the Sabbath in the strict letter of the law prescribed by the religious authorities.[41] His overriding maxim was that mercy should supersede unnecessary sacrifice and that the spirit of the law should prevail over the strict letter of the law. He modified or even abolished certain laws and rules that were no longer suitable.[42]

For a Christian, when deciding whether or not to submit to what seems an inappropriate rule or law, or even a social expectation (which can almost become an unwritten law), the highest priority is a right relationship with God. In scriptural language, this is also referred to as "living in the Spirit" and seeking the divine kingdom as a top priority.[43] It includes certain spiritual disciplines, such as prayer, meditation and Bible study, as well as putting God first in life, from which result faith,

---

[39] Mark 12:33; Matthew 12:7; Romans 14:14-23; 1 Corinthians 8:7-13; Luke 14:28
[40] John 13:15; Romans 15:5; 1 Corinthians 11:1; Hebrews 4:15-16; 12:2; 1 Peter 2:21
[41] John 4:7-27; Mark 2:15-17; Matthew 12:1-14
[42] Matthew 5:17-48; 12:1-14; Mark 7:1-23
[43] Matthew 6:33; Romans 8:4-6; Galatians 5:16; 25

wisdom, and the other fruits of the Spirit.[44] Our life overall should be subject to both divine laws and human laws. Whatever our actions, they should always be of integrity and love, as well as avoid causing unnecessary hurt. The neighbour's rights or wellbeing cannot be violated by exercising what I consider to be my rights. For example, I must not let my late-night music disturb my neighbour's sleep.

Also, I have to be true to myself and think of my own life and future. If strict obedience to my boss's demands causes me to lead a stressed, unbalanced life neglecting important priorities, including health, I must do the best I can within the given parameters. Otherwise I am obeying a person at the expense of disobeying God's principles of putting him first and looking after my body as the temple of the Holy Spirit.[45]

Considering the Consequences

Disobedience to laws of morality – those which even secular nations recognize as criminal, such as murder, sexual crimes, fraud, etc. – always has negative consequences, even if it may not be immediately apparent and may not be always experienced by the responsible party. Eventually, there will be a penalty – since everything is interconnected, the various parts affect all the other parts, and we reap what we sow. Generally speaking, we don't get away with anything. The laws of cause and effect, sowing and reaping are inexorable both in nature and in life as a whole. Even though there is divine love and grace and we can be forgiven by God for sinning, the physical results of a wrong act will need to be dealt with.[46]

---

[44] Galatians 5:16-25; 1 Peter 1:13-16
[45] Exodus 20:2, 23; 1 Corinthians 6:19-20; 10:14; 1 John 5:21
[46] Proverbs 22:8; Hosea 10:13; Galatians 6:7; 1 Corinthians 6:18

Ignoring certain other man-made rules may also have undesirable consequences. For example, if I am late for an appointment, I may miss it and have to wait or come another time, or altogether miss out on an opportunity. I may have also inconvenienced others whose appointments, following mine, are now late.

Learning to live by laws and reaping the unpleasant consequences of wrong decisions teaches responsibility and character – two vital aspects of a well-adjusted life. Children who are always protected from the results of their irresponsibility and bad choices grow up unprepared for the challenges of life. They will have difficulties in becoming productive members of the society, taking care of a family, and constructively dealing the normal problems of living that we all encounter.

What About Seemingly Nonsensical Laws?

Returning to our original question, what about laws that don't make sense to us? The truth is that we'll never be happy with all the laws and rules we are subject to. Consider for example the annoyance of waiting in long lines at the airport, then having to take off shoes, having your body scanned, open your computer, and allow a stranger to rummage through personal carry-on luggage before your vacation flight – all in the name of security and protection against terrorists. While we may not understand or agree with the rationale for certain regulations, we often have no choice but to submit – or change plans.

In some circumstances, rules can be discussed with those who made them and possibly amended. If the boss is approachable, but hasn't realized that a rule they had made is causing difficulties, they may change it if the problem is respectfully and tactfully pointed out. On the other hand, the boss may insist on his or her way and we may need to either submit or quit the job.

As far as various community laws and rules, we may be able to express our concerns to local government officials. Changes have been brought about when enough concerned citizens spoke up.

In summary, laws are intended for our good and God doesn't want his people to be in an attitude of lawlessness and rebellion. Jesus even encouraged the people in his day to obey what the Pharisees taught, even though the regulations were in part misguided and on their way out.[47] When divine laws are in conflict with human laws, the former would take precedence. Sometimes we have no choice but to submit to human laws and rules, even if they feel irksome. There are times we can try to change bad laws and regulations. And there are occasions where we can choose whether to obey or take another path, after considering the consequences of each alternative. The principles of the well-known Serenity Prayer come into play here: May we accept what we cannot change, try to change what we may be able to, and have the wisdom to know the difference.

---

[47] Deuteronomy 21:18-21; 1 Peter 2:13-20; Acts 5:29; Matthew 23:1-23

How Not to Make Things Worse

 The plumber, one of the numerous migrant workers in the Middle Eastern country where we were teaching, came to fix the leaking toilet in our apartment. After investigating for a while, he announced that a new part was needed, reassembled the unit and left.

Unfortunately, after his departure we discovered that an additional problem had been introduced, namely, the toilet was not flushing. Following another call to the Maintenance office, the plumber returned, stated that the part still was not available, but luckily restored the flushing capability. After a third phone call, thankfully a more skilled man came and fixed the leak quickly and easily without needing another part.

A few weeks later, our water heater in the small laundry area started to drip. The office sent the same unskilled plumber again. He brought a hose, unscrewed the water taps under the heater, and drained the water. However, he didn't replace the taps to close off the pipes on the now empty water heater. This omission caused water to squirt into the laundry area whenever we forgot that we couldn't use hot water and inadvertently put the tap handle near the washing machine into the warm water position. This man really seemed to have a knack for making things worse.

There are times when, despite our best intentions, we can all make an already problematic situation worse. It can be the result of wrong thinking, lack of or improper communication, as well as lack of or inappropriate action. It is therefore important to be mindful of our thoughts, words and actions as much as possible. The following examples illustrate these principles.

Thinking

All of us are prone to wrong thinking which can come in various forms such as expecting the worst from a person or situation, imputing evil motives, and judging incorrectly without having all the facts or properly understanding the matter.

Our thoughts are so powerful that they can shape our perceived and materialised reality. For example, thoughts determine whether we will succeed or fail in a project. If we believe we can't accomplish something, we'll be proven correct. The same is true in the opposite case. Studies done with school children have shown that if a teacher believed in an individual's or group's ability to succeed, the children would live up to the expectations. The opposite is also true – if we believe that a problem situation is hopeless, it will turn out to be just that.

Another kind of wrong thinking is imputing evil motives. In the case of the incompetent plumber that came to our flat, we would have made the situation worse by thinking that he was just lazy, had no character, didn't like westerners, or was spitefully messing things up. A better response would be one of compassion and kindness, believing that he is doing the best he can. Migrant workers are often overworked and underpaid, in addition to being separated from their wife and children for two or more years at a time. They sacrifice in this way so that their family back in the home country can live a little more comfortably from the hard-earned money that they send to them.

A third kind of wrong thinking is judging without having all the facts. This can then lead to unjust accusations (for example, "he/she did it on purpose") and exaggerated generalizations (such as "he/she always/never ..."), among other unsound conclusions. When these are voiced to another person, a small misunderstanding can be made into a major stand-off.

Our thoughts generate emotions which can be positive, such as love, hope and compassion; or negative, such as anger, aversion, and even hate. Thoughts and emotions affect our bodies and can make the difference between health and sickness, and ultimately life and death. That's why it is important to guard our thoughts. Wrong thoughts can indeed make numerous matters worse. Both the Bible and psychology give the following principles on sound thinking.

Become aware (mindful) of your thoughts and the fact that thoughts and beliefs make us what we are. If negative thinking becomes a habit, we'll view everything in a cynical, pessimistic way. Optimists, on the other hand, expect, and often receive, good things from life. Even when in a negative situation, they are able to focus on the positive aspects of it and make it better rather than worse. The Scriptures exhort us to focus in our thoughts on the good and edifying.[48]

Unsound thoughts and wrong desires will sooner or later manifest in improper speech and harmful actions. Since sin always starts in the mind, it is important to catch unwholesome thoughts and desires, and change them before they can do harm to ourselves and others. The Bible uses the metaphor of taking our thoughts captive and bringing them into obedience to Christ.[49]

Unhealthy and potentially destructive thoughts, against which we are also warned in the sacred writings, include covetousness and lustful desires; judging and condemning; as well as grudges, bitterness, anger, and thoughts of vengeance.[50] The antidotes are love, kindness, gratitude, contentment, believing

---

[48] Proverbs 23:7; Philippians 4:8
[49] Isaiah 55:7; James 1:13-15; Romans 1:21-28; Ephesians 2:3; 2 Corinthians 10:5
[50] Luke 6:37; Romans 2:1; 7:7-8; 13:9; 2 Corinthians 12:20; Ephesians 4:26, 31; Hebrews 10:30; James 1:19-20; 4:2

the best, and forgiveness. Refusing to forgive has been compared to eating poison and expecting the other person to die![51]

Changing our thoughts will also change the accompanying emotions. It's a matter of viewing the situation from a different perspective. Looking at a perceived enemy or scoundrel with understanding and compassion rather than with hate and anger will turn them from a foe to a fellow human who has the same needs and desires as we do, but often doesn't know how to constructively achieve them. Following the guidance of the Holy Spirit will help us to keep our unhealthy thoughts in check and to think soundly.[52]

Communication

Getting upset rather than communicating with the person concerned, or communicating with others instead, tends to make things worse. A teacher who had recently arrived from a western country became angry about his new job situation. He thought that the job expectations were unreasonable, felt that his wife's visa application was inefficiently handled, and became disheartened over the required method of teaching and the poor results. Did he talk with his boss? Unfortunately not. Did he complain to fellow employees? Somewhat. Did he ask for help? No. Instead, unbeknown to all concerned, he booked a flight and simply left the country. This not only caused initial worry about his welfare, but when the facts became obvious, also bad feelings. Chances are that after seeing the situation more objectively, he himself had to deal with some guilt issues.

Failing to honestly communicate tends to further complicate any already problematic situation. First of all, the other person

---

[51] Matthew 6:14; 18:21-35; 1 Corinthians 13:4-7; Ephesians 4:32; 5:20; Hebrews 13:5; 1 Peter 3:8
[52] Romans 12:19-21; 2 Timothy 1:7

may not even know that they did anything wrong or caused an upset. A truthful explanation regarding why we are feeling bad could lead to understanding what has, perhaps unintentionally, happened – and be followed by a sincere apology and subsequent change. Instead, the injured person becomes bitter and resentful, while the other party has no idea what is the problem. In the process, a relationship is slowly, but unnecessarily destroyed. The Scriptures, as well as wisdom and common sense, advise to resolve offences in a one-on-one interchange with the person concerned. Only if that doesn't work should other people be involved.[53]

Harsh words and anger, instead of self-control, is another way to make a bad situation worse. Likewise, overreaction and imputing bad motives instead of seeking understanding, aggravate a troublesome situation. How easy it is to get upset when things don't go our way; when unreasonable, apparently nonsensical, demands are made; or when we simply cannot understand how someone can do something so seemingly stupid. While it is natural or at least tempting to blow up, a better and healthier way is to mindfully control our emotions and stay level-headed. If at all possible, talk to the offending party – but cool off first if your emotions are boiling. Express as an I-statement how the matter makes you feel and ask some questions. It is remarkable what honest communication can accomplish. It may help you understand where the other person is coming from and what hidden pressures he or she may be under. It can also help the other party to see that their action was indeed inappropriate and as a result, an acceptable solution may be arrived at.[54]

---

[53] Matthew 18:15-17
[54] Proverbs 15:1; 25:15; 29:8,11; 30:33; 1 Kings 12:7; Ephesians 4:26; James 1:19-20

Leading people on with promises that are unlikely to be kept, in order to save face for the moment, will also in the long run poison relationships and make things worse. Trust is broken, hope is eroded, and frustration and resentment build up as a result of hurt and disappointment. The best way once again is open and honest communication – being truthful about our intentions and possibilities. Never promise what you cannot fulfil. If the situation changes to where what was possible is no longer so, let the other party know without delay. Negotiate another solution which is acceptable to both sides. This way others will not be hurt unnecessarily.[55]

Actions

Inappropriate action or neglecting to do something can be the result of ignorance, tiredness, or simply lack of wisdom or forethought. While not necessarily accompanied by evil intent, an unwise or unskilled action can have far-reaching and disastrous consequences. Planes crashed, trains collided, and ships sank with hundreds of casualties because of a wrong action (or series of actions) at the wrong time. Nuclear and environmental disasters causing untold long-term suffering have also been the result of human error.

To avoid causing unnecessary problems and pain to yourself and others, think before you act. If possible, avoid making snap decisions in times of fatigue or stress, or acting on impulse, as these actions, seen later in the right perspective, can turn out to be unwise. Good advice to follow is: measure twice, cut once; check and double check; don't rush into situations before

---

[55] Leviticus 19:11; Psalm 15:2; Ephesians 4:25; Colossians 3:8-9

thinking them through carefully; and seek advice for complex decisions and then consider all sides of the issue.[56]

Learn all you can about what you are doing and become an expert in your field. Make sure you understand the issue that you are planning to tackle. For example, if you want to help someone, make sure that the assistance you are contemplating is what the other person would like and needs. An unwisely implemented good intention can backfire and leave both parties feeling bad. In all situations, strive to deal ethically and without compromising integrity. As a principle, distance yourself from potentially compromising situations.[57]

To sum up, making mistakes is a part of being human. While errors may cause us problems, we also learn from them – and they are often stepping stones to success. However, it is easier to learn from the mistakes of others than our own, or from the wisdom others have recorded and left for us. None of us wants to worsen problems for ourselves or others. If we apply the principles of sound thinking, speaking and acting, learned both personally and from the experience of others, we will less likely exacerbate bad situations. It will also help us to resolve problems in constructive ways without needless pain and frustration.

---

[56] Remember that "fools rush in where angels fear to tread". Proverbs 11:14; 15:22; 24:6
[57] 1 Corinthians 6:18

Of Messy Houses and Loving Hearts

 On a warm summer day in Australia, about two months before Christmas, I was taking my usual morning walk. That was the first time I met the owner of the messy house that my husband and I had passed many times, wondering what may have been the problem. I used to think that perhaps an aged person or couple, no longer able to look after the house, lived there. Later I remember seeing one or two young men and assumed that they had inherited the property after the death of their parent(s).

The day I met Monica we just exchanged greetings, but then one comment led to another, and for about 20 minutes she shared with me a sizeable and tragic part of her life story. I just listened, and when she was finished, she gave me a hug and thanked me for hearing her out.

About a year away from the age of 50, Monica had had more than her fair share of difficulties, grief and heartache. They included an abusive marriage, losing two young children as a result of medical mistakes, a youngster with an immunity disorder who almost died more than once, bringing up three children as a single parent, and later having to leave her own home to protect herself from an abusive adult son.

She had moved back into her house a few months before I met her, but it had been an uphill battle to re-establish herself and regain self-esteem and confidence. Bravely, however, little by little, she had kept going, sustained by her sense of humour, active imagination expressed in poetry, a few good friends, and faith in God. She was hoping that by her 50th birthday, she would have her life reasonably together.

How easy it is to judge, and even condemn people like Monica. A messy house, overgrown garden, and furniture stacked on the front porch – what is going on? Drug addiction, mental illness, criminal activity, ...? To further add to the suspicion, in the past there were old cars in the driveway, and even a police car spotted outside the house. Surely something must be seriously wrong.

Over the weeks that followed, as I got to know Monica better, I came to see a devoted mother and a woman of integrity. While indeed struggling with serious personal and family problems, she was not only concerned for herself, but also deeply cared about others – not only her children but also needy friends.

Even though Monica's adult children had behaved thoughtlessly towards her, she always treated them kindly and remained ready to help them whenever she could. No matter what happened, she loved them, was concerned for them, and wished them well as the following example illustrates.

Monica knew she was being judged for the appearance of her house. She shared, however, that the furniture on the porch belonged to her son, John. Her brother was supposed to come and move it, but as of then hadn't. She had every right to simply get rid of it, but knowing that John had not long before injured his back and was on disability, she had not wanted to do so. Despite the abuse and grievous suffering he had caused her, Monica still unconditionally loved and had compassion for her wayward son. The door of her heart would always be open for him.

Lessons Learnt – The Folly of Judging!

My friendship with Monica, begun simply through willingness to stop and listen to a neighbour, taught me a great deal. I became more mindful of how quickly we tend to judge by appearances – instead of trying to understand and have compassion; to believe the best, rather than the worst; to be patient and seeking to find out why a person is a certain way. How swiftly we can condemn others based only on what we perceive and what we deem to be appropriate by our standards. How easy it is to jump to conclusions and to reject an individual based on appearance alone – or worse still, the appearance of their house and front yard! Yet, as I discovered, if we stop to befriend them, listen and get to know them, under the rough exterior we might find a heart of gold.

The Scriptures teach us to be careful about unwisely judging one another. In fact, we are warned that harsh judgment on our part will return to us – it is sobering to read that we'll be judged in the same manner that we judge others.[58]

Additionally, our judging is often wrong. We tend to judge by what we see, which always gives us an incomplete picture and is therefore deceiving. By contrast, God looks at the heart and knows the motives and intentions of a person.[59]

I was also reminded that there are different ways of doing things or handling situations – all or many of which may be acceptable. Much depends on the circumstances, the other person's conscience, background and experience, and most importantly, their motives. Sometimes we think that our way is the best way, or worse yet, the only way, and as a result we tend to look down on and condemn everyone who doesn't live up to our standards or expectations. We quickly jump to conclusions without having all the facts, forgetting that only God knows what is in a person's heart.[60]

---

[58] Matthew 7:1-5; Luke 6:37-38
[59] 1 Samuel 16:7; 1 Kings 8:39; 1 Chronicles 28:9; Psalm 44:21
[60] Romans 14:1-13; 1 Corinthians 4:5

Nonetheless, the Bible does stress the importance of judgment in the sense of *discernment* – but this often applies to what is right or best for ourselves and what situations we should avoid. Each person needs to practise discernment for themselves in their life circumstances. Sometimes what is right for one person may well not be the best for another.[61]

I also realize the importance of judging fairly and impartially – to be just in my dealing with others. Wrong kind of judgment can include hypocritically focusing on another person's problems, while doing the same or worse. Partiality and unjust judgment leads to failing to uphold the rights of the poor and needy. Further, I have come to see how looking at the surface of situations often fails to discern the spirit of the law and the underlying motive of love.[62]

I try to be more mindful of how I regard people who at first sight aren't appealing to me. If I can be patient and kind and attempt to find out what may be behind the seemingly unattractive exterior, I may discover a gold mine – a person sent into my life just at the right time to minister to me in undreamt of ways!

To conclude, in my dealing with others, I would like to remember the prayer of Francis of Assisi and ask: "O Divine Master, grant that I may not so much seek to be consoled as to console; to be understood as to understand; to be loved as to love."

---

[61] Proverbs 15:21; 17:18
[62] Proverbs 24:23; 31:8-9; Matthew 7:3-4; John 7:21-24; Romans 2:1-5

PART TWO: SPIRITUAL ANALOGIES FROM LIFE

Birth

Jean and Carl bubbled with excitement, joy and anticipation. Jean couldn't help but tell the whole church congregation, praising God for what had happened. After ten years of marriage, their deepest desire had been realized. A new life had begun inside her – a baby was on the way. Eight months later, a beautiful healthy girl was born. What a miracle!

Sarah and Ben were in a similar situation. They also had trouble conceiving a child that they so desperately longed for. Having tried everything medical science had to offer, including artificial insemination, finally, Sarah's pregnancy test came out positive. Again, there was much rejoicing and hope. In a few short weeks, however, Sarah miscarried and her ecstasy turned into depression. Yet a couple of years later, Sarah gave birth to a healthy boy, and only recently to his brother. She and her husband too feel very blessed.

The Wonder of Life's Beginning

The conception, development and birth of a baby are awe-inspiring. Two microscopic and very different cells (called *gametes* from a Greek word for marriage partners), one from each parent, unite to form the beginning of a new human life – referred to as an embryo, zygote, or *conceptus*. Forty-six chromosomes carry a unique combination of genetic information from both parents. The embryo, however, is far more than a set of instructions for making a new human being. Active and capable of spontaneous growth, the embryo works like several kinds of skilled craftsmen. In the proper order, it constructs the skeleton, muscles, organs, nerve connections, and a waste disposal system for the new body. In a sense, the embryo – already essentially a human being by virtue of the genes – is a blueprint, builder and house combined. In addition to the genetic information, its growth and development is also influenced by the environment – both inside and outside of the mother's body.

Inside the mother, the new life is protected from harm by a fluid-filled sac. Through the placenta – an organ to which the embryo is attached by the umbilical cord – nutrients and oxygen are transferred from the mother's bloodstream and waste products are removed from the baby's. The placenta also produces hormones to maintain the pregnancy, and then to trigger off the birth process through labour in the ninth month when the time has come for the baby to leave the womb.

The human head, body, arms and legs – even hands, feet, fingers and toes – are already formed in the second month of pregnancy, as are the eyes and ears. The cartilage skeleton also turns into bone at this stage and the baby is now called a foetus (from the Greek for young or offspring). From then the organs continue developing until birth when a miniature human being enters the world with its first cry. Those who witness a human birth, especially that of their first child, cannot help but be deeply moved by it. The biblical Psalm 139 expresses the awe of ancient King David, who did not understand prenatal development as we do, yet marvelled at God's incredible handiwork (see v. 14-16).

Spiritual Parallels with Prenatal Development

Prenatal development and birth have many spiritual parallels. In addition to the physical birth resulting in a relatively short life which ends in death, the Scriptures refer to a spirit birth, which leads to eternal, never-ending life. "You must be born again," Jesus told the puzzled Nicodemus, "not of the flesh, but of the

Spirit." The apostle Paul describes this phenomenon as "the washing of rebirth and renewal by the Holy Spirit." The divine Spirit needs to indwell a person – otherwise the individual does not belong to Christ or his kingdom.[63]

The spirit birth is in many ways a mystery and an even greater miracle than the physical birth. But the natural birth can provide a few insights as follows.

The female ovum (egg cell) has a limited life of only about 12 hours and will die unless fertilized by a male sperm. The ovum can be compared to the natural human being – created in God's image, but subject to sin and consequently to inescapable death. Without God's intervention analogous to the fertilizing male sperm, each person is destined to die after a few decades of life without any future hope. Physical conception signifies new life and a new creation, which combines the characteristics of both parents. The spiritual life, imparted by the Holy Spirit, also results in a new creation – with the human parents' characteristics and nature on the one hand and divine nature on the other.[64]

The begotten unborn baby has had nothing to do with the life-giving process. There is no effort and no choice in the matter. None of us chose our parents, time of birth, or whether we will be the first, second or third of several children. Similarly, a Spirit-begotten child of God has no say in the way God chooses to work in their life and nothing to boast about. The whole process is purely God's doing through divine love and grace.[65]

Just as an embryo and foetus develop to become more and more like a human being, and specifically his or her parents, children of God acquire more and more of their heavenly

---
[63] John 1:12-13; 3:3-8; Titus 3:5-7; Romans 8:9
[64] Romans 6:4; 8:11-14; 2 Corinthians 5:17; Ephesians 4:22-24; Colossians 3:9-10; 2 Peter 1:4
[65] John 1:11-13; 1 Corinthians 1:26-30; Ephesians 2:8-9; 2 Timothy 1:9

Father's characteristics as they grow in relationship with their Lord and Saviour, Jesus Christ. Through the transforming power of the Holy Spirit, they gradually become conformed to the image of God's Son. Over time, the fruit of the Spirit appears – love, joy, peace, patience, kindness, generosity, faithfulness, gentleness and self-control.[66]

The unborn child is already known to the parents, but not yet a visible part of the family. After birth and as they grow, all children reflect more and more of their parents' likeness. God's children, while already possessing seeds of the divine nature and eternal life, are not yet visible in their God-intended glory. As they follow the Spirit's leading and develop spiritual maturity, they are being transformed in mind and character into the image of him who redeemed them from death, called them to himself, justified them, imputed to them his own righteousness, and will glorify them with him at his second coming. At that time, the full adoption or birth into God's family will take place with "the redemption of the body" – receiving glorious immortal bodies in the resurrection. The children of God will then fully possess divine likeness.[67]

The unborn baby is developing inside the mother's body, attached to her by the umbilical cord through the placenta. The people of God too are growing and developing inside a body – the body of Christ, which is the universal church (not any particular group or denomination). Moreover, each child of God needs to be individually attached to Jesus Christ. Without this living connection, he or she is likened to a withering branch soon to be broken off. The way the placenta enables nourishment and waste removal or cleansing can be compared to how God,

---

[66] Romans 8:29; 2 Corinthians 3:18; Galatians 5:22-23; 2 Peter 3:18
[67] Romans 8:18, 22-23, 28-30; 12:2; 1 Corinthians 15:42-44, 49; 2 Corinthians 3:18; Philippians 3:20-21; 1 John 3:2

through the Scriptures and the Holy Spirit, provides nourishment and cleansing for the growing children of God.[68]

The mother carrying the baby inside her where she can best protect it can be compared to God being our protector. He is metaphorically referred to as our refuge, shelter, shield, stronghold, fortress and strong tower. Furthermore, he sends angels to surround us and protect us from dangers we may not even be aware of.[69]

Unborn children are almost totally unaware of the nature and magnitude of the world outside the womb – a world of which they are unknowingly a part and for which they are preparing. All they register are their parents' muffled voices and a few other sounds. Yet, within very small distance from the wall of the womb, there exists a large dimension, bathed in bright light, of stationary and moving objects with countless shapes, shades and sizes.

In a similar way, the physical life is a preparation for a realm that the Bible says we are not far from (and at the same time, largely unbeknown to us, we are already in it). We have been promised to enter a new dimension of God's kingdom at the resurrection from the dead. While we have an inkling about it, the glory and details of this sphere, that will include and supersede all the dimensions we exist in, are hidden from us and beyond our wildest imagination.[70]

The imminence of physical birth is signalled by the breaking of the waters. The baby no longer needs the amniotic fluid that

---

[68] John 15:1-8; 1 Corinthians 12:12-31; Galatians 4:26-31; Ephesians 4:4-7, 11-16; 5:25-32
[69] 2 Samuel 22:3, 31; 2 Kings 6:8-17; Psalm 31:2-5; 61:3-4; 91:4-8; Jeremiah 16:19; 17:17
[70] Matthew 4:17; Luke 21:31; Acts 17:26-28; 1 Corinthians 13:12; Ephesians 2:4-7; Hebrews 12: 22-24

protected it in the womb since conception as it is about to emerge into the world outside the mother's body.

Water plays a symbolic part in the spirit birth. When a person has come to repentance and accepted Jesus Christ as their personal Saviour, he or she is to undergo water baptism. The scriptural example is immersion which symbolizes death and burial of the old self – an identification with Jesus in his death. Emerging out of the water of baptism is a new person in Christ – a new birth has taken place. When Jesus accepted John's baptism and came out of the water, the Holy Spirit visibly descended on him and a voice from heaven affirmed: "This is my beloved son." The symbolism of a new birth or a resurrection as a child of God is central to Christian baptism.[71]

A newborn baby is pure and innocent – not having yet done any evil. He or she, however, is not born with a totally clean slate. We are all subject to having inherited various traits, predispositions, or even trapped emotions from our ancestors. If there are past lives, as some believe, we may bring with us into the present life those influences or certain memories as well.

Those of us who have been born again of the Spirit are forgiven and reconciled to God. We stand pure and innocent before our heavenly Father – with Jesus Christ's righteousness having been imputed to us. However, we still carry the consequences of unwise thoughts and actions from our pre-conversion life – be it physical, mental or emotional scars, some lodged deep in our sub-conscious.

Just like physical infants need nourishment to grow and develop, as babies in Christ, we need to feed on God's Word, grow in grace and knowledge, and be transformed into the divine image by the Holy Spirit (or Christ) living in us. This is

---

[71] Matthew 3:13-17; Romans 6:3-6

the process of sanctification which will continue for the rest of our life on earth.[72]

Special Births

The birth of children is a frequent theme in Scripture. At the time the Old Testament was written, children were seen as a blessing from God, while barrenness was considered a curse and disgrace. Nevertheless, barren women hold a special place in God's heart, both historically and prophetically. A dramatic reversal of barrenness even symbolizes glorious future salvation of both the people of Israel and the Gentiles.[73]

Several miraculous conceptions and births are recorded of individuals who had a unique role in God's purpose for humanity. Isaac, Jacob (later renamed Israel), Joseph, Samson, Samuel, and John the Baptist were all firstborn miracle babies. Initially their mothers had been unable to conceive naturally, and later these boys were used by God in special ways.[74]

Jesus Christ was a miracle baby in an extraordinary manner, being conceived in Mary by the Holy Spirit, rather than a male sperm. Humanly, we cannot even begin to grasp how one of the members of the divine family became God in a human body – both the Son of man and Son of God. Subject to human weakness and tempted in all the ways that we are, yet without sin, he suffered and died for the sins of humanity to be the first to be raised to glory from the dead. Fully human and fully divine, he understands and appreciates what the human experience is all about. How awesome to worship a God, who not only created

---

[72] Romans 3:22-24; 5:1-2, 9-10; 8:28-30; 12:1-10; 1 Corinthians 6:11; Colossians 1:19-23; 2 Peter 3:18
[73] Psalms 113:9; Isaiah 54:1-8; Galatians 4:27
[74] Genesis 11:30, Hebrews 11:11-12; Genesis 25:21-26; Genesis 29:31 and 30:22-24; Judges 13:2-24; 1 Samuel 1:5-20; Luke 1:7

us, but also can fully identify with us and promises to always be there for us![75]

The Bible speaks of Jesus coming in the flesh – not just the one special time through his birth to Mary, but in an ongoing manner. As through the Holy Spirit God planted Jesus in Mary's womb, after Christ's resurrection and ascension, he has been planting his divine nature through the Holy Spirit in human hearts. A miracle takes place in each case as a person previously unreceptive to God perceives and welcomes divine love and grace.[76]

As the Spirit gently leads the individual to God's Word, to a realization of his or her hopeless condition, to seeing the need for forgiveness and redemption available through Jesus' death on the cross, and to a desire for a new life with God leading to salvation, the person responds in faith and repentance and receives the down payment of eternal life.[77]

Conversion can indeed be seen as a special divine begettal or birth. Those of us who have experienced it are hidden in God with Christ as a new creation, abide in Christ, are sealed in Christ, experience freedom in Christ, and are enabled to stand firm in Christ. However, metaphorically, we are also in the process of pregnancy, having Christ formed in us, as well as being transformed into his image.[78]

As representatives or ambassadors of God's kingdom on the earth, we are bringing Christ into the world. As Jesus first came to earth in humility and without fanfare, the kingdom of God is quietly, yet powerfully, entering, and like a small piece of leaven

---

[75] Luke 2:5-7; Colossians 1:15-20; Revelation 1:5; Romans 8:29; Hebrews 4:15-16, 12:2-3
[76] 1 John 4:2-3; John 14:20; Galatians 2:20; Ephesians 3:16-19; 1 Corinthians 2:9-14
[77] Acts 11:18; Colossians 1:27
[78] 1 Corinthians 1:30; 2 Corinthians 1:21; 5:17; Galatians 2:4; 4:19; Ephesians 1:13; 4:13; Colossians 3:3

making inroads into Satan's territory. It is not always outwardly visible, but Jesus said that the kingdom of God is within – to perceptibly appear in due time.[79]

The Firstborn

The firstborn is another frequent theme in the Word of God. In the Old Testament, the firstborn child possessed special birthright blessings, being entitled to a double share of the inheritance. Such a privilege was not to be taken lightly. Esau was rejected from receiving the special blessing because he failed to value it.[80]

The last of the ten plagues before the Exodus brought death to some of the firstborn. All the Egyptian firstborn died, but every Israelite firstborn was protected by blood on doorposts – symbolically redeemed by shed blood. Soon thereafter, God decreed all the male firstborn in Israel, both man and beast, to be his. To perpetually remind the people of the great miracle before leaving Egypt, firstborn animals were to be sacrificed while firstborn sons had to be redeemed.[81]

Like Mary was chosen and especially favoured to become the physical mother of God's Son, those comprising the universal church, the family of God, are also specially selected. The New Testament shows that all who believe become the firstborn children of God and hence heirs of God and co-heirs with Christ. Having responded to God's call in their lives, they are redeemed by Christ's sacrifice on the cross and become a part of the body of Christ, as well as the bride or wife of Christ as the church is also symbolically referred to. If they remain faithful, they are promised to be in the first, or better, resurrection – the raising to

---

[79] 2 Corinthians 5:20; Matthew 13:33; Luke 17:20-21
[80] Deuteronomy 21:15-17; Genesis 25:31-34; Hebrews 12:16-17
[81] Exodus 11:4-7; 12:12-14, 17, 37-42; 13:2,11-16; 34:20

life of all the dead in Christ. For those in this resurrection, "the second death has no power over them." They are promised special positions in a glorious city full of gold and precious stones where there is absence of tears, suffering and death.[82]

God desires for all to be saved and the existence of the firstborn and first resurrection implies that others will follow. And indeed, the Scriptures allude to the "rest of the dead" being raised at a later time in a resurrection to physical life. This will include those who by God's design and no fault of theirs were not given the saving grace and knowledge of Jesus Christ during their earthly lives. They will at that time be offered salvation, and if they accept, they will receive the Holy Spirit – the seed of eternal life. While their eternal destiny may be less glorious than that of their firstborn siblings, the wondrous future that God has prepared for all his spiritually born children lies beyond human comprehension and wildest dreams. In the end, God himself will dwell with his people and all things will have been made gloriously new.[83]

---

[82] John 14:2-3; Romans 8:15-18; Ephesians 5:28-32; Hebrews 12:22-23; Revelation 14:1-4; 19:7-9; 20:4-6; 21:1-7
[83] Revelation 20:5, 11-15; 21:1-7; Ezekiel 37:1-14, 20-28

Royal Wedding

One of my Saudi students came to the office and handed me a small elongated box. Inside I found a decorated fan with writing on it. Attached to the bottom of the fan was a purple string with a tag showing my name. The student explained that it was an invitation to her friend's sister's wedding scheduled to take place in two days in the ballroom of Riyadh's prestigious Faisalia Tower.

Surprisingly for me, the starting time was 10 pm. Our Saudi neighbour translated the details of the Arabic invitation and I learned that it was a princess marrying a prince. The Saudi royal family numbers around 5000 and many young princes and princesses attend local prominent schools and universities.

My colleague, Laura, was also invited for which I was grateful. This being a female only occasion (the men would gather in another room) my husband couldn't accompany me and I didn't want to go alone, especially late at night. The invitation came as a total surprise. I believe Laura had taught the young lady last semester. With me, however, having barely finished my fourth week of teaching in Saudi Arabia and still confusing the three or four Nourahs, Sarahs and Noufs in each of my classes, I was only just beginning to know who the sister of the bride was. And I certainly wasn't one of her best teachers – still struggling to get used to the new culture and the university.

Laura mentioned that such invitations are only given to "special" people – therefore it was a real privilege. Others that my husband or I talked to about the invitation were also excited and impressed – this was no ordinary event. Saudi weddings are night occasions and go into the early hours of the morning. The couple may arrive at one or two in the morning and dinner may be served sometime after that.

Laura and I arrived not too long after the stated starting time and were among the first guests. Having been ill during the day of the wedding and missing work, Laura had left her invitation at the office. Luckily she was able to get in with just my invitation without any questions asked.

With only a few guests present when we arrived, we had a chance to walk around the ballroom, decorated in a purple and red colour scheme, and to have a good look at everything. Rows of soft chairs, covered in white and purple material, were arranged in a circular pattern around the room. A small adjacent room with a love seat was separated from the rest of the ballroom by a thin curtain. To the right of it was an area for the all-female music band with a lady singer. They soon began playing Arabic music.

As more guests arrived, Filipino ladies, who usually work as maids and servants in the country, started circulating from row to row. Attired in special purple dresses, they brought at first water, then the traditional Arabic coffee as well as mint tea, black tea, and special non-alcoholic cocktails interspersed with chocolates, popcorn, and savoury snacks. Time passed quickly with listening to music, snacking, and observing what was happening around us in this all-female gathering with young and old dressed in their best outfits.

Finally, around 1 am, the bride appeared, accompanied by dramatic music and several young girls in purple dresses. Our eyes and the cameras followed her as she slowly walked from one end of the ballroom to the other, where she finally sat on the special love seat. Many came to greet and congratulate her as she waited for the bridegroom. At last he appeared, but from our seats he was indistinguishable from the about a dozen attendants, all dressed in traditional Arab attires (long white robes with red and white checked head coverings). The procession of men joined the bride and many again greeted and congratulated the couple and the attendants. More photos were taken.

Interestingly, the groom and his attendants were not only allowed to enter the all-female party, but actually stayed for a good half hour. This was unusual because in this culture, women in public places are always covered in their abayas (long black gowns), which was not the case this evening – in fact, the dresses worn by some of the ladies were quite revealing. Also, men and women are often not allowed to wait, eat, or do business in the same area, but members of each gender have their own exclusive places where the opposite sex can't go. Perhaps at the royal level, rules are allowed to be somewhat bent.

After the main events of the bride and groom's arrival, well wishes and photographs, the female music band with the singer resumed performance – at a notch higher volume than the previously already quite loud volume. The Filipino ladies continued bringing around snacks and drinks. It was getting close to 3 am, so Laura and I thought that this could be a good time to go – though we were among the early leavers. Although we didn't see the event to the end – not knowing when the end was and having heard that it could go on for hours longer – it gave us another cultural experience and a glimpse into the Saudi society. It was also reminiscent of Jewish weddings at the time of Christ and perhaps even among Orthodox Jews in contemporary times.

Wedding as a Biblical Metaphor

Marriage and wedding are frequently used biblical metaphors. According to the Christian and Jewish Scriptures, marriage was instituted at Creation and the first wedding would have occurred before humanity's separation from God (known as "the Fall").[84]

In the Old Testament, the relationship between a man and a woman pictures the relationship between God (who was Jesus Christ before his incarnation) and the nation Israel. It was to be marked by life-long loyalty and faithfulness. Unfortunately Israel failed to honour their covenant with God and went into idolatry. As a result, God in Christ terminated the relationship and after his death on the cross, entered into a marriage covenant with the church. In a relationship with God, idolatry is closely paralleled with spiritual adultery.[85]

The gospels include several wedding references. Jesus performed his first miracle at a wedding that he and his family were invited to. When the wine ran out, he created more from water. Several of the kingdom of God parables revolve around weddings. Matthew's gospel describes ten virgins, five wise and five foolish, waiting at night for the bridegroom who is delayed. When he finally arrives, the wise virgins are ready to meet him, while the foolish ones are not. Luke describes servants expected to faithfully perform their duties while their master goes away, gets married, and returns from a wedding. They will then be treated to a special banquet.[86]

The Marriage of Jesus Christ

The Bible also mentions a very special wedding invitation – far surpassing any on this earth. This extraordinary event, figuratively portrayed as a royal wedding, is not just a prince and a princess marrying in an earthly kingdom. The King of Kings and Lord of Lords, the glorified Jesus Christ, who will establish his

---

[84] Genesis 2:21-25
[85] Jeremiah 3:8-14; 1 Corinthians 10:1-5; Romans 7:4; Ephesians 5:23-32
[86] John 2:1-11; Matthew 25:1-13; Luke 12:36-38

heavenly kingdom and rule over all the earthly kingdoms, will be marrying his glorified, righteous church whom he has redeemed with his blood on the cross. God the Father himself is organizing the wedding and the children of God will have a part in it, but not earned by what good they have done or what they may deserve, but rather by grace or special favour.[87]

Like my invitation to the Saudi royal wedding, this invitation is unearned and undeserved. Surprisingly, it may go to those who are not even seeking the Divine and are unworthy as far as any personal merit before God is concerned.

For example, some of the Gentiles were given the opportunity to get to know the Divine without anything special that they had done, while Israel, who sought God through their own righteousness, did not find him. Also, those who were invited, but treated the invitation lightly – being too busy with other matters – were replaced by those picked up from the streets. While incomprehensible to our limited minds, one day we will be given understanding of such divine mysteries.[88]

While my colleague, Laura, was lucky to get into the Saudi wedding without her invitation card, the heavenly royal wedding will not be entered without a divine invitation. Only those who are called, chosen and faithful, who have the Holy Spirit residing in them, and who have the garments of Christ's righteousness will be allowed to enter.[89]

New Testament wedding parables picture the coming kingdom of God where there will be no more gender differences or individual marriages.[90] We do not know the exact details how it is all going to fit together, but we can perhaps speculate a little. There is likely to be far, far more than snacks and coffee, but

---

[87] Ephesians 5:22-32; Revelation 19:7-9
[88] Romans 9:25-33; 11:7-11; Matthew 22:3-13
[89] Matthew 22:3-13; 25:1-12; Revelation 17:14
[90] Matthew 22:30; Luke 20:34-36; Galatians 3:28

perhaps a sumptuous meal of unimagined exquisiteness will be enjoyed by all. Men and women will not be segregated, but all together will enjoy the direct presence of Jesus Christ, for in God, all are one. Angelic choirs and orchestra may well provide celestial music in every sense of the word. Whatever the details, one thing is certain: the wedding of Jesus Christ and the church will be an indescribably glorious and happy occasion, far surpassing any royal wedding on the earth.

May we all take care not to be too preoccupied with the concerns of this world, to remain faithful servants of God, and to be ready when the bridegroom returns, so that we will, through the grace of God, be worthy to be there.

Death of Two Young Men

On Tuesday, David celebrated his 35th birthday. A brilliant young man, he had a doctorate in physics and was pursuing his second one in Christian education. In addition, he pastored a church, served as a chairman of a Christian society, and was engaged to be married with the wedding planned in two months. To those who knew him he was a helper, a spiritual mentor, and an inspiration. On Friday afternoon he went for his usual run. He never returned. During his exercise he collapsed and died. In one moment, all his plans and aspirations came to an end.

Shocked and devastated family and friends are trying to come to grips with the tragedy. It seems so unreal and unbelievable – like lightning from a clear blue sky. Why did God allow this to happen? Death is always an enemy, but why a young man in the prime of his life? And one who had been such a dedicated servant of God and fellow humans?

These heartrending questions highlight something most people struggle with – the notion of death. We know in theory that it will come to each of us and to all our loved ones sooner or later. Yet, unless we have lost a family member or a close friend, we prefer not to think about it, to live in denial – almost pretending death doesn't exist.

Death of Another Young Man

The Scriptures speak of another young man in his thirties. He too was specially gifted by God, a Christian educator teaching God's way to multitudes, and engaged to be married (figuratively speaking). He was likewise a servant of God, dedicated to unconditionally doing his heavenly Father's will.[91]

He led and mentored a group of young men whom he envisioned would in turn, together with their disciples, one day influence the whole world through their sharing the knowledge of a soon-coming divine kingdom. He taught, healed, and in many ways helped to meet people's physical and spiritual needs. He even brought three people back to life.[92]

People had great hope in him – they expected him to proclaim himself the king of an earthly kingdom and to deliver them from foreign oppression. One Sunday, he triumphantly entered Jerusalem and accepted the people's praise and adoration. The following Friday, he was dead. Those who had admired and lauded him a few days earlier had him crucified. Above his head was placed a sign reading "Jesus, the King of the Jews."[93]

His friends and followers were confounded and overwhelmed – indeed devastated as all their hopes were crushed. His inner circle of disciples seemingly began to forget all that they had experienced in their three and a half years with him as they were planning to return to their former occupations.[94]

A couple of days later came another shock. The tomb where he had been laid was empty – the corpse had disappeared! Then, an even more inconceivable and stunning event – Jesus appeared to them alive! None of them could doubt it! It was him, standing among them, now risen from the dead! He had tried to tell them that it would happen this way, but at the time they simply couldn't grasp it.[95]

---

[91] See Matthew 5:1-7:28; Ephesians 5:25-32; Revelation 19:6-9; John 6:38; Matthew 26:39-42
[92] See Matthew 24:14; 28:18; Luke 7:11-16; 8:40-56; John 11:1-44
[93] See Matthew 21-27
[94] See Luke 24:13-35
[95] See Mark 8:31-33; Luke 24:36-45

Hope in the Face of Death

Death remains a real and formidable enemy. All of us have encountered it directly, through losing loved ones or indirectly through the media or hearsay. Parents have lost young children to illness or accidents, newlyweds have lost partners in wars, adults will lose their aging parents – people die at all stages of life and for countless reasons.

Encouragingly however, the Bible tells us that Jesus Christ has conquered death and brought news of eternal life and immortality. A day will come when there is no more death, sorrow and mourning.[96]

Those who have died having the Spirit of Christ working in them will be resurrected – as will also those who have died without knowing God. Just like Jesus called Lazarus, the brother of Mary and Martha, as well as the Nain widow's son and Jairus' little daughter back to life while on earth, he will return from heaven and call all his deceased followers – and eventually all others – out of their graves.[97] David, the Christian worker, will be among the resurrected and be reunited with those who loved him. In the meantime, he has left a legacy that will inspire others to follow in his footsteps till the glorious time of the resurrection.

Jesus died for the cause of a great good for many. Through him, all may potentially receive forgiveness, justification, and ultimately salvation and eternal life. While the reasons for and benefits of an untimely death of a loved one may remain a mystery, God promises that all things work together for good for those who seek and love him.[98]

We all have a magnificent hope that death is not the end. Just as Jesus rose from the dead to a new life of glory, humans are

---

[96] See 2 Timothy 1:10; Hebrews 2:14-15; Revelation 21:4
[97] See Romans 8:11; Daniel 12:1-2; 1 Corinthians 15:12-26; Ezekiel 37:1-14
[98] See Hebrews 2:8-11; Romans 3:21-26; 8:28

likewise destined to be raised from their graves to a perfect, eternal existence in unspeakable joy.[99] May our present sorrowing for deceased loved ones be tempered by the hope of that wonderful time!

---

[99] See 1 Corinthians 15:44-58; 1 Thessalonians 4:13-18

Freeing the Prisoners

The small group of believers gathered to study the Scriptures mused about how times have changed. Not many years ago, they would not have been allowed to get together as a group without an ordained leader presiding over the meeting. They would certainly not have been permitted to voice their opinions about faith matters, let alone discuss the sacred writings and form their own conclusions. They have grown up bound in fear of a literal ever-burning hell in which those who refused to unquestionably submit to the authority of their organization were destined to suffer for eternity. Now they felt free to even express how wrong all that indoctrination was, how they were all kept in a dark dungeon of deception, and what damage it has done to their psyches.

Imprisonment to religious dogmas and fear is only one type of captivity. This essay explores other ways in which we are bound, suggests means to free ourselves, and points to an already present as well as coming universal liberation program.

A Captive World

The world abounds in situations of undue control and oppression of various kinds. Totalitarian regimes with rigid ideologies – be it forms of communism, military dictatorship, or even fundamentalist theocracy, among others – persecute, threaten, imprison, torture, or even kill those who disagree and publicly express their own views. People are brainwashed by cleverly devised propaganda. Independent thinking is strongly discouraged and a childish dependence on the governing machinery is promoted.

Millions of people are imprisoned in hopeless poverty, mindless jobs, involuntary prostitution, destructive relationships, substance addictions, compulsive behaviours, dysfunctional minds or bodies, fears and phobias of all kinds, stressful daily grinds to make ends meet, as well as literal soul-destroying prisons where many are held unjustly. The list could go on and on. These and other circumstances are situations of real or virtual slavery.

It is true that some oppressive regimes have changed or are changing. Political prisoners have been released and there is a greater freedom of expression than before in some countries. Democracies with free elections have replaced oppressive dictatorships in a few cases. However, sadly, even that doesn't guarantee true freedom.

History shows that a leader can be democratically elected, as was for example Adolf Hitler, and in a few years turn into an insane despot enslaving the inhabitants of numerous countries. It took a bloody World War with millions of lost lives, as well as untold damage to property, infrastructure, and human psyches, to bring about liberation from the Nazi/Fascist regime of the last century. And even then, only a short time later, hundreds of millions were imprisoned again – this time for over four decades – under oppressive Communism. In many cases, as is so poignantly illustrated in George Orwell's *Animal Farm*, the liberated oppressed soon become the new oppressors.

While there is ever-increasing awareness of and much talk about human rights and freedom at high levels of governments and even in the United Nations, the issues of the poor remaining poor or becoming poorer are also still realities. Exploitation and abuse of workers in developing countries continues, with women and children being especially vulnerable. Even in developed nations, domestic violence and child abuse are a scourge, as are alcoholism and drug addiction. Despite amazing advances in science and technology, it seems that humans are incapable of bringing about a just society where all are free to use their God-given talents and live in conditions conducive to developing their true potential. Why is that?

Based on the Holy Bible, which I believe still has relevance for post-modernity, I would like to propose that throughout history, the whole world has been held captive by a power or being outside of the human sphere. All people are to a smaller or greater extent under this influence, and of and by their own efforts are unable to free themselves from it. On a positive note however, the Scriptures also give hope that liberation is coming and indeed, is already here for those who become aware of it.

About the Captor

The biblical record mentions a mighty spirit being of superior intelligence that in eternity past, before humanity's existence, chose to oppose and go contrary to God. While giving little specific information, the Scriptures allude to Satan the devil's origin as that of Lucifer, or light bringer, who served at God's throne. Desiring self-exaltation, Satan alienated himself from God, becoming the adversary and personification of evil. He was followed in his apostasy by a large number (possibly a third) of angels, now referred to as demons. With their help, Satan keeps the world in darkness from which it can and will be delivered through God's plan for salvation.[100]

Scriptures refer to the devil in many ways including as the enemy, evil one, murderer, liar, thief, tempter and accuser. The Bible states that he has been sinful from the beginning and is in active pursuit of destroying the people of God – those who by

---

[100] Isaiah 14:12-14; Ezekiel 28:12-15; Acts 26:16-18; Colossians 1:13; 1 Peter 2:9; Revelation 12:4-9

grace have been enlightened and follow the ways of God. Through his influence on human minds, Satan can fuel animosity, strife and hate among individuals and nations. He has deceived the whole world, is a destroyer, and holds the power of death.[101]

Even though God is overall sovereign, throughout human history, Satan has been allowed to occupy a rulership position over the earth. He is referred to as the god of this world, ruler of darkness, prince of demons, and "ruler of the kingdom of the air." In charge of the "abyss" or underworld, he is the source of highly destructive spiritual influences.[102]

Scripture also mentions numerous angels who sinned, left their appointed place, abandoned their positions, and followed Satan in his rebellion. As demons, they too are negatively influencing the world, sometimes seeking to possess people or even animals. During his earthly ministry, Jesus Christ cast demons out of many people and empowered his servants to do likewise. Satan and the demons are all waiting for judgment and punishment at a future time, after which their destructive influences will cease.[103]

How the World Is Imprisoned

Satan uses at least three approaches to keep the world under his sway and control. Firstly, he lies and deceives; secondly, he entices and seduces; and thirdly, he forces and coerces.

Called the father of lies and liars, the devil is a master deceiver. The entire world lies under his deception. Counterfeiting

---

[101] Zechariah 3:1-2; Matthew 4:1-11; 13:38-39; John 8:44; 10:10; 1 Thessalonians 3:5; Hebrews 2:14; 1 Peter 5:8; 1 John 3:8; Revelation 12:9-17
[102] Job 1:12; 2:6; Matthew 12:24; Luke 4:4-7; 2 Corinthians 4:4; Ephesians 2:2; 6:12; Revelation 9:1-11
[103] Matthew 25:41; Mark 1:34; 5:12-15; 6:13; 16:9; 2 Peter 2:4; Jude 6; Revelation 9:14-15; 12:7-9

the truth, he subtly leads people into false beliefs and wrong actions. According to the creation story (a mythical narrative with inherent spiritual truth), Satan, disguised as a serpent, deceived Eve and caused the fall of the human race in the Garden of Eden. Posing as an angel of light – a role from his former existence – he misleads people into actions that seem right, but are out of line with divine instructions. He can use magic – impressive signs and wonders – to delude. Satan also accuses, defames and slanders, thereby insinuating and disseminating untrue derogatory information about people or even God. Influencing people's thoughts and words, he is a master at creating doubts and suspicion, destroying reputations, and setting humans against each other.[104]

The devil's second approach is seduction. Cunning as a serpent, he is able to charm his victims, tempt them to sin, and lead them to ruin. He subtly lures people into false values, such as power, possessions and selfish ambition, which will draw them away from God. Craving personal worship, his goal is to cause humanity to serve and worship him while thinking they are serving God.[105]

Thirdly, Satan uses force and violence. As a liar, destroyer and murderer, he can lead people to hate and kill, and even drive a person to the unnatural act of suicide. Pictured as a dragon and a roaring lion, Satan can instigate threats and intimidation toward those he hates. He can also distress with grievous and long-term sickness and disease. Through "fiery darts" and oppression of the soul, he can torment people emotionally and mentally, and

---

[104] Genesis 3:1-5; Job 1:2, 10; Proverbs 14:12; 16:25; Matthew 24:24; John 8:44; 2 Corinthians 11:3-4; 13-15; Galatians 1:6-9; 1 Timothy 4:1-3; 2 Timothy 3:1-8; Revelation 12:10; 16:14
[105] Matthew 13:38-39; Luke 4:1-8; 1 Thessalonians 3:5; 1 Timothy 4:1; 2 Timothy 2:26; Psalms 91:3

even possess them. Finally, Satan can unleash violent weather and other natural disasters.[106]

Deceived and ignorant, humanity has also used force and violence against their source of physical sustenance, "Mother Earth". Foolishly and short-sightedly, nature has been recklessly exploited, polluted and raped by those with insatiable appetites for gain. Many living creatures have been mercilessly hunted, some almost out of existence. Farm birds and animals are cruelly mutilated, and then imprisoned in tiny cages and enclosures during their short lives while drugged and force-fed in order to bring maximum profit to the meat industry. The results have been upset balance on numerous fronts resulting in the extinct-tion of some species; overpopulation of other, often destructive, species; rise in human and animal sickness and disease; as well as destructive weather and other natural disasters.

Our Responsibility and Way Out

While we are influenced by an all-pervasive external spirit power, we also need to take responsibility for our own thoughts, words and actions. Each of us has had a personal part in causing hurt and suffering to others around us – be it family, friends, and even strangers. We have gotten angry, acted thoughtlessly, said unkind words, been selfish to those in need, and more. This has brought suffering not only to others, but to ourselves as well.

Once we begin to perceive and understand what is happening, why we think negative, unloving thoughts and act in hurtful and destructive ways, we can do something about it. If we admit these failings and the harm we have caused and resolve to change, we'll be on our way to freedom – at least partially. As

---

[106] Job 1:14-19; 2:7-8; Daniel 10:13; Matthew 24:9; 27:3-5; Luke 13:11-16; John 16:2; 17:14; Ephesians 2:2; 6:13-16; 1 Thessalonians 2:18; 1 Peter 5:8; Revelation 9:2

we, with divine help, learn to habitually practice kindness and compassion to others and ourselves, our prison doors will start opening and we'll feel happier and more joyous.[107]

By becoming increasingly aware of our thoughts and reactions – through a process called mindfulness – we can be on guard against those that produce negative results. As we align with the leading of the Holy Spirit, by divine help, our lives will be gradually transformed into the likeness of Jesus Christ. We'll become less grasping and attached to situations and things, and more easygoing; less intent on gaining power, status and wealth, and more interested in spiritual values; and less desirous of increasing material possessions and more generous.[108]

Hope of Ultimate Liberation

While the devil is mighty and his efforts are widespread and destructive, whatever he does is nonetheless limited through God's almighty power. In total sovereignty, God redeems Satan's activities to accomplish divine purposes on the earth.

Jesus Christ, as God incarnate, was ordained to be born as a man, experience all that is common to humanity, and die for human sin. During his earthly ministry, he preached hope of liberation through the establishment of the kingdom of God. He brought enlightenment (liberation from darkness) to those who were able and willing to receive it. He also freed many from the prisons of sickness, demon possession, and social stigma. And because of his human experience, he understands and can help those in need. Finally, through his death and resurrection, he empowered his disciples to continue the ministry of liberation – to eventually encompass the whole world.[109]

---

[107] Acts 20:21; 26:20; Luke 3:7-14; 4:18; 2 Corinthians 3:17
[108] Romans 12:2; Ephesians 4:22-5:4; Colossians 1:21; 3:2-10
[109] Isaiah 42:7; 49:8-9; 51:14; 61:1; Luke 4:18; 10:17-19; Mark 1:29-34; 3:10-11; Hebrews 2:10-18; 4:14-15

Jesus personally overcame and defeated Satan and destroyed Satan's work by overcoming sin and death. As a result, those who are able to accept him as their Lord and Saviour respond by turning to God, asking forgiveness, and following the divine way of love. "Born again" through the power of the Holy Spirit, they are liberated from sin and therefore need not fear death any longer. Instead, they can be encouraged in the hope of eternal life. The Scriptures teach that in God and Christ there is freedom. Jesus has set people free from sin, deception and death.[110]

Much of the world is still in darkness and held captive. However, as the divine kingdom is making inroads, prisoners are being freed through truth and action of the Holy Spirit. Those who embrace the light of God are beginning to taste freedom. Liberation is taking place here and now as the omnipresent divine Spirit enlightens minds and changes lives.[111]

Jesus Christ promised to return to the earth. At his second coming, he will fully establish the kingdom of God by taking over earthly kingdoms now ruled by Satan. Physical and spiritual prisons will be opened wide, and those who have languished there for so long will finally be unbound and set free. Ultimately, when Satan is forever removed, true knowledge will cover the earth and there will be no more deception, suffering and death. All will be free and living in harmony as everything becomes new – and of the increase of the divine government and peace there will be no end.[112]

---

[110] John 12:31; 16:11; Romans 6:16-22; 8:1-11; 2 Corinthians 3:17; Galatians 2:4; Colossians 2:15; 2 Timothy 1:10; 1 John 3:8; Revelation 1:5-6
[111] Psalm 116:16; John 8:31-32; Galatians 5:1,13; Colossians 1:21-22; Hebrews 2:14-15; 1 Peter 2:16
[112] Matthew 24:30; John 14:3; Acts 11:1; Revelation 1:7; 11:15-18; Isaiah 2:2-4; 9:6-7; 11:1-10; Matthew 25:41; Revelation 20:10,15; 21:1-7; 22:1-6

Coming to Life on Facebook

Some time ago I joined the world of Facebook – the social networking website where people find old friends and make new ones. As I registered and wrote down one of the places where I worked in the past, faces of long ago started appearing. Checking friends of the people I knew, I discovered other familiar names and faces. I was finding people that I had lost contact with and have occasionally wondered how their lives had gone over the last few years or decades, or how certain issues had worked out. When I requested to join their friendship list, I received messages such as: "Great to hear from you. Been thinking of you from time to time and of the good times spent together. How has your life gone over all these years?"

Facebook offered to find other friends through my email address book. Faces from a more recent past appeared, as well as present ones that I have only occasional contact with. There they all were with their unique life stories. Many had pictures with snippets of their lives, such as marriage partners, travel, children or grandchildren. Searching for some other friends yielded no results. They have not yet joined this new technological world with its amazing ability to reunite old friends from all parts of the world and bring them face to face – even if only through the computer.

My search is not over yet – I can continue it at periodic intervals as I revisit Facebook. I have to yet explore friends of those I have known and am sure to find other mutual friends there. This finding of old friends and acquaintances may be an almost endless process and after a certain point, it will become impossible to keep up with all the people I have known.

As I update some old friends on how I believe God has worked in my life – like a weaver creating a beautiful tapestry that only he knows the final pattern of – I look forward to finding out what has happened in their lives since I last saw them.

Seeing someone again, even if only in cyberspace, brings forth a flood of memories – of good times as well as trying times. We are carried in our minds back years, even decades, ago to a different time and place. Other associations come to mind and with them certain emotions – both happy and sad. Everything has been amazingly stored in our memories and the subconscious. Bringing it to the surface can also be a time of healing in our own minds if some issues had been buried without proper resolution at the time.

These cyberspace reunions also make me reflect on what I perceive as analogies with spiritual realities that the Bible gives us glimpses of regarding our future reunion with loved ones in the kingdom of God. I will explore these in what follows.

Spiritual Analogies

Facebook is said to have about one billion users. If these people can be seen as representing the world's population, God would know each of them by name. He also knows them intimately, caring and providing for every single one's needs, even though he may not be known or acknowledged by them. Through special grace and at a certain time, however, he touches some people's lives, opens their minds, and invites them to share in his love and friendship. (All will be given this opportunity at one time or another.) If they accept, they get a glimpse into God's nature and plan of salvation. They can then start building a relationship with the Creator God and his Son, Jesus Christ, who died to become their Saviour. They become friends of God and much more – amazingly, the Scriptures calls them children and heirs of God and co-heirs with Jesus Christ.[113]

Another analogy comes to mind. If those on Facebook were to represent the people of God – those called and enlightened, who have accepted God's invitation – then, by inviting each other into their friendship circles, they build ties as members of the family of God, God's household, and the citizens of the heavenly kingdom, who will one day follow Jesus to full glory.[114]

My little reunion with old friends in cyberspace may also in a minute way give a glimpse of the reunion in the resurrection at Jesus' return to earth. The Bible mentions that Jesus Christ is preparing places for his followers and will in the future bring back to life and receive those who have died in faith. The symbolism of a wedding banquet is used. While in this life we cannot even remotely comprehend our ultimate glorious destiny, we can use the imagination to keep our hope alive – being certain that whatever we picture in our minds will be exceedingly superseded.[115]

At the time of Jesus' return in his glory, those who have responded to God's drawing, been born again, and have the Holy Spirit as a deposit of eternal life are promised to be resurrected to immortality and given glorious incorruptible bodies. A reunion of the faithful presently living, as well as those who have died in the faith both recently and long ago, is pictured. Ultimately, life of unimaginable joy and fulfilment is alluded to as the saved will live with God in the new heaven and new earth for all eternity. Gone will be all suffering, tears, sickness and death.[116]

---

[113] Matthew 5:44-45; John 6:44, 65; 15:12-17; Acts 5:30-32; Romans 8:13-17
[114] Ephesians 2:12-19; 1 Timothy 3:15; 1 John 3:1-2
[115] John 14:2-3; Ephesians 3:19-21; 5:31-32; 1 Thessalonians 4:13-17; Revelation 19:7-9
[116] Romans 8:9-11; 1 Corinthians 15:42-44, 49-54; Revelation 21:1-5

The Wedding Banquet

The following scenario of the divine reception and wedding banquet is obviously speculative. However, since imagination is all we have for now, let's just dream a little.

Perhaps after being raised from the dead and given eternal life, we'll all stand in a long, but glorious receiving line. While we move forward to be personally welcomed by our Lord, Saviour and King, Jesus Christ, we'll notice familiar faces around us. We may hug and kiss, maybe even shed a few tears of joy at the incredible fulfilment of our long-awaited hope, and we may also share our life stories since we had seen each other.

We may hear tales of joy mixed with stories of sadness – learn about joyous births and untimely deaths; success stories as well as those of tragedies and disasters; love relationships as well as difficult or broken relationships; health and fitness interspersed with sickness, injury, perhaps even incapacitating illness, and finally death. Also a part of many lives will have been experiences of God's special interventions, such as protection from serious harm or untimely loss of life. In the cases of pain and suffering, the sense of God's presence and help will have been felt.[117]

Time – if there will be a sense of time in the new sphere – may pass quickly and before long, we'll be near the beginning of the receiving line where Jesus himself stands in all his glory and splendour. After his hearty welcome and commendation,[118] angels may escort us to the banquet table. Each person may have a special seat reserved for them.[119] And seated next to us and on the opposite side of the table may be other friends that we had lost contact with during our physical lives. Happy reunions will

---

[117] Hebrews 13:5; Psalm 22:1-5; 34:4-10; 97:10; 2 Corinthians 1:9-10
[118] Matthew 25:20-23
[119] Mark 10:36-40

be occurring all around as family members separated by death are finding each other.

There will be young people who had never met their grandparents or great-grandparents. Perhaps the extended families will all sit together at the table – though some would need a very big table to accommodate all their relatives! Laughter, tears of joy, and relief that all the pain and suffering is finally over will pervade the banquet atmosphere. There may, however, also be a tad of sadness if a loved one is missing.

We don't know how long this indescribable banquet will go on or even what meaning, if any, time will have. In Old Testament times, wedding feasts lasted a good part of a week and we are told that in God's sphere a thousand years is like a day.[120] Perhaps after we have become reacquainted with our nearest loved ones, we'll circulate, find others we have known, and join them in another part of the banquet room for some catching up. Perhaps we'll discover the missing person. Perhaps we'll have the privilege to talk to Jesus or God the Father or the Holy Spirit and ask some questions. All things will be possible in the new realm where everyone will just want to please, praise and glorify God. For each person, there will be many others to catch up with or get to know anew. The task in all likelihood won't be completed during the banquet, but we'll have all of eternity to do it.

Of course, this picture may turn out to be nothing like the actual reality as we are dealing with incomprehensible mystery and the Bible only gives us, through symbol and metaphor, fleeting glimpses of the Ultimate in ways that we can get our limited minds around.

---

[120] Psalm 90:4; 2 Peter 3:8

Those Not at the Banquet

If we don't find the missing loved one, perhaps Jesus will explain why. There may be a sad, but valid and just, reason why they are not at the banquet and in the kingdom of God. On the other hand, maybe all is not lost. The Bible alludes to a first resurrection and those called in this life, together with Jesus, being referred to as firstfruits. This implies another resurrection and another harvest of souls. And indeed, the Scriptures allude to these as well. This opportunity, possibly a thousand years or some period of time later, would only be given to those who because of no fault of theirs, but by God's design, were not enabled by grace during their earthly life to come to the Saviour, receive the Holy Spirit, and be born from above.[121]

Whichever way it will be accomplished, God desires all humans to be saved by grace and all will be given an opportunity – in God's way and time. Ultimately, all God's decisions and judgments will be seen as right and just.[122]

We may choose to put our name on Facebook and enjoy sharing snippets of our life with others. However, only God can in his sovereign timing and grace place our name into the Book of Life. Once our mind has been opened to understanding of our part in the process of salvation and we have received the Holy Spirit, we need to remain faithful to God's way of life. Then, on the Day of Judgment, our names will be in the Book of Life and we'll be invited to the great reunion at the marriage of the Lamb.[123]

Reconnecting with old friends and acquaintances through the technology of Facebook can help us, in a very small way, imagine

---

[121] Romans 8:22-23; 1 Corinthians 15:21-23; James 1:18; Revelation 14:1-5; 20:4-6; Ezekiel 37:1-14
[122] 1 Timothy 2:3-6
[123] Philippians 2:12, 4:3; 2 Thessalonians 2:13; Revelation 3:5; 13:8; 17:8; 19:7-9; 20:15; 21:27; 22:19

reconnecting with those we have known in the future kingdom of God. While the picture I have painted is obviously speculative, it can give our limited minds something to grasp on to keep our future hope alive. In whatever way it will happen, let's all look forward to seeing each other, together with those who have preceded us in death, all glorified and immortal, at the great wedding supper of the Lamb.[124]

---

[124] Matthew 22:2; 1 Corinthians 15:42-54; Revelation 19:7-9

About the Author

Eva Peck has a Christian and international background. Through Christian work as well as teaching English as a second language in several countries, she has experienced a range of cultures, customs and environments. Having lived and worked in Australia, the United States, Europe, Asia, and the Middle East, she now draws on those experiences in her writing.

Eva refers to biblical passages in this book the way she has come to understand them. Having had the opportunity to fellowship with Christians from a variety of faith traditions, she also recognizes that many faith-related issues can be understood in more than one way.

Eva studied biological sciences as well as theology at the tertiary level and has Bachelors degree in science and a Masters degree in Theology. She lives in Brisbane, Australia, with her husband, Alexander. The Pecks' other books of spiritual nature include *Pathway to Life – through the Holy Scriptures* and *Journey to the Divine Within – through Silence, Stillness and Simplicity*. Both publications, as well as Eva's trilogy *Divine Reflections* can be ordered online through Pathway Publishing at www.pathway-publishing.org. For more information about Pathway Publishing, see page 101.

More About the Author's Other Books

Divine Reflections in Times and Seasons

This book looks at times and seasons and explores how everyday phenomena mirror spiritual realities. Readers are encouraged to take a fresh look at a sunrise, the sunlight on trees and flowers, the creatures that cross their path, and the starry heavens, among other things, and contemplate the meaning of it all.

Divine Reflections in Natural Phenomena

This book explores how spiritual realities can be glimpsed in the world of nature – in phenomena such as life and its order, the beauty and harmony around us, and the countless mysteries of the heaven and the earth.

Divine Reflections in Living Things

This volume looks at living organisms among both plants and animals and reflects on the glimpses of the divine in these realms. Readers are encouraged to pause and take a fresh look around them – to see each living creature and every process as if for the first time.

Pathway to Life – Through the Holy Scriptures

Pathway to Life presents in a concise and systematic way the basic teachings of the Bible. It strives to offer a balanced, non-denominational understanding of the Scriptures. Conclusions are supported by scripture references.

Journey to the Divine Within – Through Silence, Stillness and Simplicity

Journey to the Divine Within shares, through the reflections of a variety of spiritual writers, how to enter the realm of one's heart. One way that this occurs is through silence, stillness and simplicity. When pondered, the reflections will lead readers to the silence and stillness of their own hearts on the path to encountering the Life, Light and Love within.

Other Resources

Eva Peck has created several websites with spiritual content. Feel free to browse and explore.

Truth & Beauty
(www.truth-and-beauty.org)

This site seeks to capture what is true and lovely. With the aim of helping readers appreciate the nature of Ultimate Reality, it deals with practical and spiritual aspects of life. To uplift and edify, it provides galleries with beautiful nature images as well as heart-warming stories.

Pathway to Life
(www.pathway-to-life.org)

The site presents the essential Christian message under 36 biblical topics in Q & A style. Where several denominational views exist regarding a subject, these are covered as different interpretations. Supporting scriptures are given throughout. The information is also available in book form.

Heaven's Reflections
(www.heavens-reflections.org)

The site features the theme of seeing the extraordinary in the ordinary, the sacred in the daily, and the special in the routine. It focuses on how the world around us, upon deeper looking, reflects spiritual realities. This book, as well as the *Divine Reflections* trilogy is based on the content of the website.

You may also enjoy visiting Alex's websites:

Spirituality for Life
(www.spirituality-for-life.org)

The site shares information with the aim of presenting a practical spirituality to enhance one's life journey and to help fulfil one's divine destiny.

Prayer of the Heart – Journey to the Divine Within
(www.prayer-of-the-heart.org)

This site deals with the prayer of the heart or meditation, covered from a mainly Christian perspective. It features quotations from a variety of spiritual writers. The content is also available in book form.

About the Artist

After a successful music career, my father, Jindrich Degen, returned to art, a hobby from early in his life. Now, at 90 years of age, he has a large portfolio of diverse paintings, many of which are abstract and symbolic. I have selected three of them for this book.

Those further interested in Jindrich's artwork will find more information and pictures on his website, www.henrydegen.com. The website also includes his photography and poetry (in Czech). His art, photography and poetry are also available in book form.

About Pathway Publishing

Pathway Publishing is dedicated to sharing truth and beauty by publishing books that present what is true to life and reality, as well as what is lovely and inspirational. The goal is to not only provide sound information, but also to lift the human spirit.

Pathway Publishing has a vision of helping readers on their path of enlightenment and spiritual transformation. The wisdom and experience of spiritual teachers, thinkers and visionary writers from various backgrounds and faith traditions are recognized and valued.

Books produced by Pathway Publishing besides *Divine Insights from Human Life* include:

- *Divine Reflections in Times and Seasons,* Eva Peck
- *Divine Reflections in Natural Phenomena,* Eva Peck
- *Divine Reflections in Living Things,* Eva Peck
- *Pathway to Life - Through the Holy Scriptures,* Eva and Alexander Peck
- *Journey to the Divine Within – Through Silence, Stillness and Simplicity,* Alexander and Eva Peck
- *Artistic Inspirations - Paintings of Jindrich Degen* arranged by Eva and Alexander Peck
- *Floral and Nature Art – Photography of Jindrich Degen* arranged by Eva and Alexander Peck
- *Memories of Times with Dad – Poems and Letters,* Alexander and Eva Peck
- *Volné verše,* Jindrich Degen (in Czech)
- *Verše pro dnešní dobu,* Jindrich Degen (in Czech)

Some of the publications are also becoming available as e-books.

Pathway Publishing
Seeking truth and beauty

www.ingramcontent.com/pod-product-compliance
Lightning Source LLC
Chambersburg PA
CBHW031258290426
44109CB00012B/634